Poppy

Book and lyrics by
Peter Nichols

Music by
Monty Norman

Samuel French - London
New York - Toronto - Hollywood

Poppy was first published in 1982 by Methuen London Ltd

ISBN 0 573 08086 0

Please see page iv for further copyright information.

POPPY

Poppy was first performed by the Royal Shakespeare Company at the Barbican Theatre, London on 25th September, 1982. The first performance of this revised version was presented at the Half Moon Theatre on 25th August, 1988, with the following cast:

Obadiah Upward	Edward Clayton
Sally Forth	Nicky Croydon
Tao-Kuan, Emperor of China	David Fielder
Chorus	Siobhan Finneran
Chorus	Kate Hamilton
Lin Tse-tsii	Ayub Khan-Din
Dick Whittington	Josie Lawrence
Queen Victoria	Tina Marian
Chorus	Jon Osbaldeston
Chorus	Amanda Rosen
Lady Dodo	David Ross
Chorus	Scott St Martyn
Jack Idle	Gary Shail
Chorus	Michael Strassen

Directed by Chris Bond
Designed by Ellen Cairns
Lighting by Jim Simmons
Musical director Stewart Mackintosh

CHARACTERS

Emperor of China
Queen Victoria
Jack Idle, a manservant
Randy, his horse
Sally Forth, a schoolmistress
Cherry, her mare
Lady Dodo, the dowager Lady Whittington
Dick Whittington, the squire
Obadiah Upward, a London merchant
Lin Tse-tsii, Commissioner to Canton

Chorus of Villagers, Clerks, Indians, Bearers, Servants, Animals, Mandarins, Guards

SYNOPSIS OF SCENES

MUSICAL NUMBERS

ACT I

	Overture	
Music 1	Opening	Chorus
Music 2	Whoa, Boy	Jack, Sally
Music 3	The Good Old Days	Dodo, Dick, Chorus
Music 4	In These Chambers/When I Was A Lad	Upward, Clerks
Music 5	If You Want To Make a Killing	Upward, Dodo, Dick
Music 6	John Companee	Dick, Jack, Victoria, Indians
Music 7	Nostalgie de la Boue	Dodo, Upward
Music 7A	We Sailed Downstream	Clerks, Victoria
Music 8	Poppy	Dick, Sally, Jack

ACT II

Music 9	Bounty of the Earth	British, Mandarins
Music 10	They All Look The Same To Us	Lin, Chorus
Music 10G	Whoa, Boy (*reprise*)	Jack, Sally
Music 10H	Whoa, Boy (*reprise*)	Dick, Sally
Music 11	In These Chambers (*reprise*)	Clerks, Dick, Upward
Music 12	The Blessed Trinity	Upward, Dick, Victoria, Sally
Music 13	Sir Richard's Song	Dodo, Sally
Music 14	Rock-a-Bye, Randy	Jack
Music 15	Kow-tow	Dick, Chorus
Music 15C	The Treaty	Sally
Music 16	Chinese Takeaway	Dodo, Upward
Music 17	Finale: Bounty of the Earth (*reprise*)	Company
Music 18	Finale: Blessed Trinity (*reprise*)	Company

Vocal Score and orchestral parts are on hire from Samuel French Ltd

ACT I

Overture

Scene 1

Prologue

During the orchestral overture, the front tabs rise to show a swirling mass of clouds and water. A place where gods and emperors can meet

The music takes on an oriental tinge and Lights come up behind the scrim. A gong is struck. We hear voices intoning:

All	From the paradise of countless
Women	trees
Men	From the paradise of countless trees
All	In the shade of the Temple of Universal Joy.

Gong

Men	Hear the greeting of Tao-Kuang,
	Emp'ror of the Middle Kingdom,
Women	Son of Heaven,
	Ruler of the Four Seas,
Men	Glorious rectitude,
	Lasting glory,
Women	Glorious rectitude,
	Lasting glory,
All	Glorious rectitude,
	Lasting glory,
	Glorious rectitude,
	Lasting glory.

Gong

The Emperor has gradually appeared during this. Robed and splendid in a throne floating high above. He should perform magic before he speaks: a live dove from his sleeve would be wonderful

Emperor	Our Dragon voice, at which all subjects quake
	Now thunders at the Hour of the Snake
	Across our vast domains by magic wiles
	To bid our regent of The Western Isles
	Approach our throne with all humility.
	Now, humble king, are you receiving me?

More thunder and flares. The Emperor conjures up Victoria in a cloud of smoke

Forgive us, are you sure you are a king?
Your tribal garb is so bewildering,
Your head-dress and regalia so wild,
You seem to us more like a female child.

Victoria Maiden we may be but—though still a minor—
By grace of God, Victoria Regina.
We rule not only England, Scotland, Wales,
But——

Emperor Please don't weary us with travellers' tales.
Who cares who rules these lands we understand are in,
A semi-savage state?

Victoria Look here, your mandarin
Deserves a reprimand, he's got it wrong——

Emperor Come, child, this audience is getting long.

Victoria (*With a glance at the house*)
This audience is being sorely tried,
They want their queen to speak and say with pride
We have an empire growing every day——

Emperor Enough! Hear our decree. Your people may
Continue sending toys—
Although the guns made rather too much noise

Victoria We're glad you were amused.

Emperor Amused? Not we.
Monarchs aren't easy to amuse.

Victoria I see.

Emperor As long as you instruct your envoys now
Never to come again without kow-tow.

Victoria That's not a word we British over use.

Emperor Nine knockings of the head close to my shoes.

Victoria In groups of three.
Our subjects bow
Or go down on one knee. They don't kow-tow.

Burst of threatening music. Gong

Emperor Vain girl, you'd better learn kow-tow chop-chop.
Or else you'll find we've shut the China Shop.
Without our tea and rhubarb your whole nation
Will die in agonies of constipation.
We tolerate this trade through our complaisance
As long as envoys make the right obeisance.
To anyone who won't we'll close our doors.
Young queen, we've said enough. The choice is yours!

More noise, music and smoke. A last gong

   The Emperor vanishes

Victoria (*to the audience*)

Do Chinamen always behave that churlish
Or is he shocked to find someone so girlish
Wearing Britain's crown? Well, we'll find out.
He'll keep on dropping in, I make no doubt,
And I'll pop up, to stop you all complaining
You came tonight for something entertaining.
Not boorish arrogance from Lasting Glory.
But pretty girls, true love, a fairy story.

English pastoral music, including church bells

And hark! The English church-bells softly chime
To start the story. Once upon a time
There was a village far from London Town,
That called itself Dunroamin-on-the-Down.

SCENE 2

The Courtyard of Whittington Manor

A ramshackle house behind, neglected outbuildings with thatched roofs, beams and gables; behind them part of a Gothic chapel with a crooked weathervane; in the courtyard near a statue are a well and a tree

Jack Idle comes from the stables, carrying a saddle. He's in his twenties, bright, hard-working, speaks with a cockney accent. He leads Randy, a pantomime horse

Jack (*coming* C) Whoa, boy. Stand at—ease. Stand easy.

Randy collapses on the last command

I said "stand". You haven't forgotten how to stand have you?

Randy shakes his head emphatically and whinnies, stands, scrapes his hind hoof on the stage several times

Now, now, that's enough of that. In front of all the boys and girls. Hallo, boys and girls. My name's Jack Idle. Whenever I say "Hallo, boys and girls" I want you to say "Hallo, Jack." Can you do that?
Audience Yes.
Jack Let's try. Hallo, boys and girls.
Audience Hallo, Jack.
Jack You'll get better as the night wears on. And on. And on. Oh, this is Randy. Say hallo to the boys and girls.

Randy curtsies

Collapsing like that before we've even started our journey. Oh I forgot to tell you.

We're off to London—yes The Smoke,
Because Dunroamin's stoney broke;

> Someone's started an Industrial Revolution,
> And moving to London's the only solution
> Leaving our village to live in the town,
> Because Dunroamin's on the Down.

Mind you, I was born in London. Yes, I was a cockney sparrow till the day I flew away. And Randy was a totter's horse, weren't you, me old mate?

Randy nods

Not much of a life was it?

Randy shakes his head

And now we're happy where we are, eh?

Randy nods

Shall I tell them why, the boys and girls?

Randy shakes then nods, confused

> Why should we seek a favourable breeze
> To carry us to the Antipodes
> When all our heart's desire is in this valley—
> A mare called Cherry and a girl called Sally?

He looks about

> But look, old sport, they've left us all alone—
> A chance for me to play my xylophone.

He pulls a xylophone from behind a tree and nods to the orchestra conductor

Thank you, Professor.

As the band plays the opening chords, the Chorus enter

The orchestra changes and plays Sally's intro instead

> *Sally enters, the principal girl, in Victorian riding gear*

Jack puts away his xylophone

Sally Hallo, Jack. Hallo, Randy.
Jack Hallo, Sally.
Sally (*to the audience*) Hallo, boys and girls.
Audience Hallo, Sally.
Sally And I'm sure you'd all like to see my little Cherry, wouldn't you? Come along, Cherry.

> *Cherry enters, a glamorous mare with long lashes*

Jack has to hold back Randy who's scraping the stage with his hoof

Jack Down, boy, down, before I do you a mischief.

Sally and Jack stand between the horses

Sally (*taking his arm*) Oh, Jack, I was afraid I'd miss you, afraid you'd have gone.

Jack Would that have mattered?

Sally Oh, Jack, of course it would. Aren't we the best of friends? And didn't you want to kiss goodbye?

Randy has crept round behind and is mounting Cherry, who whinnies and tries to shake him off

Jack Randy, Randy, get down this minute!

He goes upstage and pulls Randy down. The mare trots to Sally

Behave yourself!

Sally There, there, Cherry, never mind. (*To Jack*) She's blushing.

A red spot on Cherry

Jack Greedy, that's his trouble. I mean, it's not as if he hasn't had his oats today. (*He shouts at Randy*) Three bags full you've had already. You're a dirty—filthy—uncontrollable—length of pox-ridden lechery. I should have let you go to the knackers' yard. It's all you're fit for. (*He tethers Randy to the well*)

Sally (*with Cherry but to Jack*) Leave him alone, Jack. I won't allow you to chastize him like that. You might hurt him.

Jack He's got to learn.

Sally I'm the village schoolmistress. You don't teach by cruelty but by example.

Jack Yeah, well he's a fine example in front of all the boys and girls.

He looks at the audience. Sally comes down, leaving Cherry

Sally (*to the audience*) Perhaps they can help us. Listen everyone if you see Randy moving again, shout "Whoa, boy". Will you do that? Will you?

Audience reaction

Oh thank you. (*To Jack*) Oh, Jack, they say they will, I think they're going to be on our side.

Jack (*shielding his eyes against the lights, looking out, dubiously*) You reckon? Well, we're gonna need some help and all.

Sally We certainly are. If we're to get rid of the old farmyard England——

Jack And learn to hide our feelings——

Sally In spite of the way they insist on showing . . .

She takes his arm flirtatiously. The orchestra plays the intro but either the audience or the conductor stops the music because Randy is moving across to Cherry. As they turn, Randy stops, innocently looking about. They play a few games with this, then Cherry comes down to Sally and Jack goes to untether Randy. If the audience didn't help:

Jack (*returning with Randy*) Lot of help they were. (*Of the audience*) There's a lady up there shouting—"Go on, Randy".

Sally Self-control is what we need. Thank you, Professor.

The intro plays again and they sing, each to their animals. This also includes dancing with the horses.

Music 2: Whoa, Boy

Jack

Whoa, boy
No, boy
Slow, boy.

Sally

Hey, girl.
Nay, girl,
Stay, girl.

Jack

You know you've got a crush
When blood begins to rush,
No-one can miss the blush
On your face
You'll have me in disgrace
So whoa, boy,
No, boy,
Slow, boy.

Sally

Hey, girl.
Nay, girl.
Stay, girl.
'Cos all that wild fluctuation
In your circulation
Is a clear indication
How much you care.

Both

So whoa, there.
No, there.
Slow, there.
I can't take you anywhere.
So however it's hurting
Hide it from view
Till the moment you're certain
That the raging desire
That's got you on fire
Is burning her too

Jack   Then go boy
Sally   Go girl
Jack   Glow boy.
Sally   Heigh ho, girl.
Both   You'll never, never, never say no
No mo'!

At the end of the song there is loud gunfire off stage. The Chorus cries out. A large bird falls on to the stage

Sally, Jack and the horses run off

The Chorus hides

There is another bang and a hunting horn sounds

> *Dodo, the Dame, enters. She is played by a man and wears hunting gear hung about with dead animals and carries a smoking shotgun*

Dodo adds the last bird to her bag

Dodo Anything that moves I put a bullet in, and that includes you, boys and girls. My bag so far today—three rabbits, a brace of pheasants, a wild duck, a seagull, a cherry orchard, and a spokesperson from the Friends of the Earth. Little boy sit still, sit still dear, or you shall feel the rough edge of my tongue—you lucky person. You have been warned.

> *Jack and Sally enter*

The Chorus emerges. Jack and Sally mingle with them

Jack }
Sally } *(together)* Good-morning, Lady Dodo.
Dodo Oooh, you could frighten anyone to death, jumping out like that. What are all these people doing in my back garden? Aren't they a load of commoners?
Sally Yes, Your Ladyship.
Dodo Then why aren't they on the common?
Jack Your son invited them, Lady Dodo.
Dodo Lady Dodo? Lady Dodo? I am the Dowager Lady Dorothea. Don't you even know what a Dodo is, you half-witted, D-stream, comprehensive school bumpkin? It's a hideous extinct old bird.
Jack We know that, Lady Dodo.
Dodo Get off my land, the lot of you. Yobs, *paysans*, *putains*! *Sacré bleu*!
Sally But, Lady Dodo, they were all asked to come here by the young master to say goodbye. He himself is off to London to seek his fortune.
Dodo Why, why, why, I ask myself. Where did I go wrong?
Jack Don't ask yourself. Ask your son——
Sally Because here he comes!

> *Dick Whittington enters, the principal boy, played by a beautiful young woman. He is wearing black but it's a tight-fitting suit with high-heeled shoes and legs in tights reaching nearly to his shoulders. He's putting on black leather gloves and carries a riding crop*

Dick Good-morning, boys and girls.
Chorus Good-morning, squire.
Dick Good-morning, Sally.
Sally *(curtsying)* Good-morning, sir.
Dick Good-morning, Mother.
Dodo Good-morning, son.
Dick I didn't see you at breakfast.
Dodo No, I was out shooting lunch. Is it true you invited all these commoners here?
Dick Is that what you call them?
Dodo They couldn't be much commoner if they tried.

Dick They are the villagers.

Chorus Aaarrrr.

Dick For centuries the faithful servants of our fine old family.

Chorus Aaarrrr.

Dick But how have we rewarded their loyalty and labour? Dunroamin's in ruins.

Chorus Aaarrrr.

Dodo And whose fault's that? It's theirs.

Dick Oh, no it's not.

Dodo Oh, yes it is.   }
Chorus Oh no it's not. } *(Repeated twice)*

Dick Within a year I promise you I'll see our family thrive again, or my name's not Dick Whittington.

Dodo A Whittington in trade! We'll never live this down.

Dick But Mother, the first Dick Whittington, who thrice became Lord Mayor of London, was up to his neck in trade. Fairy tales are no use in the new Victorian age that's coming. Britain's going to have to go out into the market-place, find new customers, sell more goods, compete with other nations.

Dodo He talks like a young upwardly mobile professional person already.

Dick That's the only way there's any hope of living happily ever after.

Dodo After? We lived happily before. In the good old days. Ask them, if you don't believe me. Weren't you? Happy before? In the good old days?

Dodo sweeps them with her gun. They eagerly agree

Music 3: The Good Old Days

(Singing)	Now let us praise
	The good old days,
	The life of Riley and the easy ways,
	When everybody knew their station—
	The golden age before we had inflation.
	For half a crown
	You'd buy a gown,
	A trip to London where we'd paint the town,
	Champagne, oysters and the fare both ways
	In the good old days
	(With some left over).
All	In the good old days—
Dodo	We were in clover
All	In the good old days
Dodo	Don't you agree?
Dick	No.
All	In days gone by
	When pigs could fly
Dodo	And no-one had to swallow humble pie.
All	There was no common cold or rabies
Dodo	And hanky-panky didn't lead to babies.

Boys	The beer was free
Girls	And so were we!
Boys	Half-naked girls lay under every tree.
Dodo	The men knew how to stop them catching cold
	In the days of old—
Dick	Now pull the other!
Chorus	In the days gone by—
Dodo	Believe your mother!
All	In the good old days!
Dodo	A tradesman! Your father will be turning in his grave.
Dick	Well, Mother, I'm the squire now
	And rather than a slave,
	I'll be a tradesman any day. It's absolutely vital
	To pay our debts
	And bring new honour to our ancient title.
(*Singing*)	Stop pining for
	The days of yore!
	Believe me, there are better times in store.
	The age of gold's not past, it's coming:
	With roses round the door.
Dodo	And inside plumbing!
All	It's gonna be
	A century
	Of daring British ingenuity
	With other nations standing by amazed
	In the good new days.
Dodo	We'll have a carriage,
All	In the days to come,
Dodo	A double garage?
All	In the age of steam?
Dodo	And no more marriage!
All	In the good new days.

Dick, Jack and Chorus exit

Dodo He's right you know, Sally. It's time to think positive. I'm still a young woman with my whole life before me. I shall assemble my ensemble de voyage.

Sally But where are you going, Your Ladyship?

Dodo To London. On business.

Sally But, My Lady, has it occured to you? In London you may come across Dick.

Dodo Well, I wouldn't have put it quite so bluntly but—yes I certainly hope so. Well where can you find any round here? You can go for a tramp in the woods but they're very quick on their feet these days and nine times out of ten—oh you mean my son?

Sally Did I say Dick? I meant Jack, of course.

Dodo A slip of the tongue.

Sally Yes.

Dodo Easily done.

Sally Oh, My Lady, let me come with you.
Dodo No, no.
Sally I've got enough money for both our fares.
Dodo Yes, yes.
Sally (*aside*) The school milk money. It can be a loan.
Dodo Well, why not? We'll call you my chaperone.
   (*Aside*)   My chic will be more stunningly displayed
                 Beside the rustic look of the poor maid.
                 (*To the audience*) *Au'voir paysans, à bientôt*, toodle-oo.
                 And don't do anything I wouldn't do.

SCENE 3

Obadiah Upward's office

Cloth flies revealing a city office: a window with a view of St Paul's, portraits in oils, chandelier, desks

The music becomes the intro to a Gilbert and Sullivan sort of song. The preamble is sung by four Clerks with quill pens, ledgers, abacuses, etc

Music 4: In These Chambers

Clerks

In these chambers fine and spacious
Verging on the ostentatious
Sits a merchant perspicacious
Obadiah Upward.

In our time few business men shall
Be one whit as influential,
So we beg a reverential

Silence for the most courageous
Man the city's seen for ages.
(And what's more he pays our wages!)
Obadiah Obadiah Upward. Upward Upward.

Upward's revealed at the main desk: he's fifty, robust, prosperous, hearty

When I Was A Lad

Upward

When I was a lad of ten I went
And worked as a grocer's assistant:
My present condition eminent
Seemed rather more than distant
But at my trade I did so well
That the promised land grew closer.
I loved to buy and I loved to sell
So I finally bought the grocer.

Clerks	He was bought with ease like a pound of cheese That old-established grocer. Upward, upward, ever upward, How your business grows! Selling flutes to poor deaf mutes And ice to Eskimos.
Upward	I bought a failing partnership And profits started mounting Because I never lost my grip On checking and accounting A fair young maid was now my wife— I'd bid for her and bought her— But sadly she went and lost her life Giving birth to our only daughter.
Clerks	Well, she wasn't much fun and her job was done Giving birth to his only daughter. Upward, upward, clever Upward Watch him while he flogs Coconuts to native huts And woolies to the wogs.
Upward	But still my upward-looking eyes Are fixed on something higher. By far the most elusive prize Is being made a squire. I'd ride a hunter with such verve That when I came to mount her They'd none of them guess I used to serve Behind the bacon counter.
Clerks	It blows our mind that he stood behind A common-or-garden counter. Obadiah, ever ever upward, how do you make so much?
Upward	'Cos I'm so bold and turn to gold Everything I touch. For I love to buy
Clerks	My oh my!
Upward	And I love to sell
Clerks	Well well well!
Upward	I'm glad my occupation is trade
Clerks	That's where his origins are displayed
Upward	And this is the tale of the life so far of
Clerks	Obadiah (*8 times*)
Upward	Obadiah, Obadiah, Obadiah.
Clerks	Ooooo . . . . h Obadiah.

Upward   Upward!
Clerks   Yeah!

Upward Work!

Dick enters

Dick At your service sir.
Upward Who are you, sir?
Dick Dick Whittington.
Upward That rings a bell.
Dick I am the only son of the late Sir Richard Whittington, heir to the estate and all his debts.
Upward S'welp me bob! So the old man's dead. I'm sorry to hear it. The man to whom I owe my prosperity. These pretentious premises, the chandelier. Well, what can I do for you, sir?
Dick Sir Richard settled a gaming debt of yours and afterwards wouldn't suffer you to repay him. Five hundred pounds? And here, sir, is your IOU.
Upward Because I was in trade, he told me.
Dick Papa was a thumping snob all right.
Upward But you're not?
Dick About trade? No. Makes the world go round.
Upward And you've come for what's yours? Only too happy.

Jack enters

Jack Hallo, cockney boys and girls.
Dick Jack Idle, my man of all work.
Jack (*touching his forelock to Upward*) I had to leave Randy outside on a yellow line. A copper was taking numbers.
Upward Cratchit, slip some money to the Old Bill.
Dick The Old Bill, who's that?
Jack The bobby.
Dick Are Bobby and Old Bill the same?
Upward Bobby, Old Bill, Peeler, Blue, Law, Rozzer.
Jack Policeman. Cockney slang.
Upward But you shall have your money anyway, Sir Richard, if it was my very last monkey.
Dick Cockney slang?
Jack Five hundred pounds.
Dick I want to be paid in kind, not cash. I want a position in your business.
Upward S'welp me bob, I'd be chuffed beyond words to have your moniker on my notepaper. Give my enterprise enormous catchit.
Dick Would it?
Upward You wouldn't knob it. I lack class. Tone. A noble seat. And have the poppy anyway.
Dick The poppy?
Jack Cockney slang for money.

Dodo and Sally come on

Dodo Well, where's this thieving skinflint Upward?
Dick Mother!
Dodo Dick!
Jack Sally!
Sally Jack!
Dick What are you doing here?
Dodo This is your father's address book. I'm looking for a tradesman called Upward, one of the crooks who ruined the House of Whittington.
Dick This is Mr Upward and he's no robber but an honourable City merchant who's about to suggest a position for me.
Dodo I'll bet he is!
Dick And here's his five hundred pounds.
Dodo For that much I'll suggest a few positions myself. (*She lifts her skirts and puts the money among her petticoats*) And he is quite dishy. What exactly is your business m'sieur?
Upward I tend these days to deal only in lines that do good.
Dodo A do-gooder? I can't bear them. *Guardian* readers, Liberal voters and the sort of drop-outs that want to prohibit blood sports.
Upward S'welp me bob, I should hope not. No, business is a blood sport.
Sally We haven't seen much blood in the City.
Upward That's because it's shed elsewhere. When I said do-good, I meant medicinal, health-giving, pleasurable.
Dodo (*ogling*) Meaning . . . ?
Upward Poppy, for instance.
Dodo (*disappointed*) Poppy?
Dick Slang for money.
Upward No, in this case I mean opium.
Dick Is there much poppy to be made from poppy?
Upward It's a nice little earner. Here in England it's made into a liquid called laudanum—or Baby's Mixture. Or Infant Quietness.
Sally And that's how it does good?
Upward Why, miss, it's nothing less than the oil that keeps the wheels of industry turning. How d'you think those working women spend twelve hours a day in the factories? D'you suppose they take their babies in?
Dick I'll wager they put them out to nurse.
Upward And how d'you think those old crones keep them quiet when they cry to be fed?
Dick With a spoonful of soothing cordial?
Upward And another. Then another. A nice little earner, as I said.
Sally It seems the village school ma'am's got a lot to learn.
Upward And as for abroad, that's another story. I sail with the tide for foreign parts.
Dodo *Quel dommage!* And we've only just met.
Upward Why don't you come along madam, and bring your son with you.
Sally Oh no! I mean—Jack too?
Dick My ward, Sally.
Upward Well why not bring all your family?
Jack I'll go and get Randy.

Upward I'm sailing in a merchantman with a cargo of Lancashire cotton goods bound for Bengal.

Sally The Indians buy them? I've always taught that they make their own.

Upward They used to. And threatened to wipe out British textiles altogether, the local labour being cheap as dirt. Then our mill owners rationalized their operation, got the kiddies into the factories, even cheaper than the blacks. Bingo! Made our goods competitive once more in the world markets.

Dick It's the right attitude for a new age.

Upward At Calcutta we board one of my own clippers, with an altogether different cargo, bound for Canton in China.

Dick How's that strike you, Sally? The fabulous coast of Cathay?

Sally Aladdin's cave?

Upward Right, miss. And we have the Open Sesame.

Upward and the others sing

Music 5: If You Want to Make a Killing

(*Singing*)
> If you want to make a killing
> And you're capable and willing,
> Then your pockets you'll be filling
> In Cathay;

> And in regions oriental
> A determined occidental
> Will be treated in a gentle-
> Manly way.

> Which is why I'm now a shipper
> With a record-breaker clipper
> And a mile-a-minute skipper
> On his day.

Dodo
> I suppose that if you carry tea
> With any regularity
> You'll never be to charity
> A prey?

Upward
> But a man would be a silly'un
> Who thought he'd make a million
> From tea or from vermilion
> Today.

Dick
> If the chinks are the suppliers
> And we're forced to be the buyers
> That can hardly justify us
> In our stay?

Upward
> For I know there is a line a
> City man has found much finer
> And it's one for which the China
> Man will pay:

                          In Calcutta grows a crop he
                          Can't resist in any shop; he
                          Loves the product of the poppy
    (*Speaking*)   What d'say?
Dick What do we say? Hooray and let's away!
Dodo You mean we're taking poppy? A shipful of money?
Jack No, ma'am. Opium.
Dodo I'm confused.
Jack It's not easy to tell the difference, (*to the audience*) is it, boys and
    girls?
Dick   What can we lose?
Dodo   A widow's cruise—
Upward   A bit of trade—
Dodo   Perhaps some jade—
Sally   A far-off land—
Jack   Us, hand in hand—
Sally   A Chinese demon—
Dodo   Lot of seamen!
All   (*singing*) Let's be on our way

                            SCENE 4

Victoria and the Emperor

*The principals go aboard and the ship makes its way across the stormy ocean
to India*

The Emperor appears in thunder and lightning

Emperor I, Son of Heaven, master of the Four Seas, view with alarm your
    mariners' efforts to attain the Middle Kingdom.

Victoria enters

Victoria You should know our navy rules the waves. Our captains are
    masters not only of Four Seas but all the others too.
Emperor (*creating thunder and lightning*) Silence, girl! You are but the
    female potentate of a rugged tribe of red-haired clansmen living in houses
    built of clay.
Victoria And you are—dangerously misinformed.
Emperor You destroyed India!
Victoria We are a modern trading nation.
Emperor Trading! What was once a land of plenty, you turned into a field
    of weeds. Where once grew the fruits of the earth, you planted only the
    flowers of dreams. You made the dark-skinned people slaves.
Victoria They were heathens. They fought each other like dogs. We brought
    them peace. And Christian reason. And Colonel Clive. We brought them
    the famous East India Company. Or as we like to call it—John Company.
Emperor A gang of savages.

Victoria A company of gentlemen.

Emperor Gentlemen—do not tear up rice, corn, cotton, and spice and force farmers to sew poison. Gentlemen don't enslave nations. Gentlemen don't deal in death or bring goods at gunpoint.

Victoria Perhaps a visit from the British and Foreign Bible Society could throw some light—

The Emperor throws a thunderbolt

Emperor No more missionaries. No more traders, bringing trash and trinkets no-one wants. No growth of trade with the Middle Kingdom. No more Foreign Shit!

Victoria I beg your pardon.

Emperor Opium. This trade must cease. Do not incur our wrath! Remember we are known as Lasting Glory.

He vanishes with full effects

Victoria waves away smoke

Victoria   My claim's more modest, I'll be England's Glory,
A match for anyone. Oh, what a bore he
'S proving. Still, if he didn't pop up, how we'd miss him!
Next time he comes on, why not boo and hiss him?
Meanwhile Dick and his friends have travelled far,
To India, up the Ganges to Bihar.
It's more than time the Son of Heaven knew
My countrymen can build an empire too.
Another trick the panto utilizes;
Fairy Queens in various disguises.

Victoria changes into a missionary's dress

SCENE 5

India. A schoolroom in an opium plantation

Victoria, Jack and Dick are on stage with the Chorus who now play Indian natives

Victoria Bus. Chibberow. Chup I said. Now settle down boys and girls but sit up straight, eyes front, pay attention. We are lucky enough to have an English gentleman to help us with our lessons today—Ram Krishna, not listening—he is Sir Richard Whittington.

Dick And his man of all work Jack.

Jack Hallo, Indian boys and girls.

Victoria And he is going to tell you all about the history of your own wonderful country.

Dick Thank you, Miss Fortune. Well boys and girls I hope you realize just how lucky you are to have Miss Fortune as your teacher. And to have this splendid school out here in the open air where all around us grows the marvellous flower that makes it all possible. And who can tell me what it's called?

Victoria Anyone?

Jack (*if necessary*) It's on the front of your programmes.

Dick The Poppy, yes. But this is no ordinary poppy is it? This is the marvellous *Papaver Somniferum*. The wonderful, health-giving, peace-giving Opium Poppy. And I've just been looking at the fields where it grows. Where your parents plough and weed and water and drain it. And where one day you too will work, slitting the seed cases, harvesting the gum as it oozes from the pod for three weeks, an ounce a day. I'll wager it takes all the patience of timeless Asia and although two pounds a year may not sound like a lot of wages to us in the West I dare say it's wealth indeed to your mums and dads. But it wasn't always like this was it, Miss Fortune?

Victoria No indeed boys and girls, because once upon a time your foolish native princes quarrelled over this land like dogs over a bone, didn't they and reduced it to a bloodstained wilderness and Sarojini Veeraswamy will know nothing about all this if she goes on staring into space. Neither will she know anything about the infamous Black Hole of—where, anyone? Calcutta, yes. An atrocity that was soundly avenged by—yes?—no-one remembers? They don't even know their own history, Sir Richard.

Dick Colonel Clive, boys and girls, don't you forget it. Suraj-al-Dowlah got such a hiding at the Battle of Plassey *he* never did for sure.

Jack My grandad fought at Plassey.

Dick Did he by George. I'll wager he had some tale to tell.

Jack He said he got very wet.

Dick He did more than he knew. He set India free. Free to become the most dazzling of the great and growing circlet of jewels that comprise the Empire. Free to develop her greatest natural asset. *Papaver Somniferum.*

Jack Oh. I thought the East India Company owned all the poppy.

Dick Yes; of course John Companee OWNS it, but the natives DEVELOP it.

Jack Oh yeah; that's where the two pounds a year comes in.

Dick Exactly. But without men like Colonel Clive and your grandad none of this would be possible. They gave these people the Pax Brittanica! And now the cup has passed to us. An awesome task.

Dick and Jack put on red coats, etc.

(*To the audience*)
> For years we'll find The White Man's Burden crippling,
> Until it's clothed in words by Rudyard Kipling.

Music. The Indians listen in the manner of supers in operetta. They may join in the martial chorus

Music 6: John Companee

Dick

The English came as Buccaneers,
Greedy, free and bold;
They won from the enemy privateers
A share of India's gold.
Men of the shires brought to their knees
The Spaniard and the Gaul
So Hun and Dutch and Portuguese
All had to quit Bengal,
Seen off by the upstart Island few
Who set the natives free,
Protecting the Muslim and Hindu
Within a company, within a company

Jack }
Dick } *(together)*

John Companee, John Companee,
Comes at first protectively,
Rescues you from tyranny,
One more child sits on the knee
To swell the growing family
Of John Companee,

Jack

I signed on as trooper with the bloomin' infantry
It was either that or starvin', so I served the
        Company:
Hardly started shavin' when I took the sergeant's
        shillin'
First they learned me buglin' and then they learned
        me killing.

Shipped East, we wus, before I knew a Gyppo from a
        Chink
And as for Injuns, blimey, they was all as black as
        ink.
Then it was "Idle, where's my boots?" and "Idle,
        fetch my flamin' grog"
For there was no-one lower down than me except a
        wog

A sweeper name of Ram; so it was "Ram, you
        itherao,
Fetch Idle sahib's boots, you heathen dog, so Juldi
        jao."
He salaamed me as he oughta but I loved the
        so-and-so
For we wus both untouchables, the lowest of the low.

**Jack, Dick
and Victoria**

John Companee, John Companee,
Comes at first protectively,
Rescues you from tyranny,
One more child sits on the knee
To swell the growing family
Of John Companee.

Dick

The English clime is none too warm,
They settle somewhere sunny,
Appearing such a languid swarm
That all may share the honey;
But beware, e'en as you smile
At their manners droll
They'll show you quite another style
The minute they're in a hole.
Remember the foolish native king,
Who dared disturb the hive,
Remember the vengeful, mortal sting
Of Plassey and of Clive, of Plassey and of Clive.

Jack, Dick
and Victoria

John Companee, John Companee
Comes at first protectively,
Rescues you from tyranny,
One more child sits on the knee
To swell the growing family
Of John Companee.

Jack (*speaking*)

I never knew the reasons why, just the flamin' facts.
I sez to Ram, "Tikh Hai," sez I, "We're off to fight
      the blacks."
At Plassey it was "In the trench and lay like you was
      dead"
While the enemy artillery thundered over'ead
No sooner had that left off when the monsoon rain
      came fallin'
And sergeants cried "Each man his gun hide under a
      tarpaulin!"
Whereby we kept dry powder while they their powder
      spent
And, when the rain passed over up we got and in we
      went.
Outnumbered ten to one we wus but all their guns
      was damp
So not a shot was fired from Suraj-Al-Dowlah's
      camp
And several of his muckers was uncommon cowardly
Which meant we conquered India in decent time for
      tea.

All (*singing*)

John Companee, John Companee,
Comes at first protectively,
Rescues you from tyranny,
One more child sits on the knee
To swell the growing family
Of John Companee.

Dick

But low, thou hast a purpose seen,
Purged of sneer and boast,
Marching to an anthem clean
Sung by a godly host—

	Take up, take up the white man's cross,

Take up, take up the white man's cross,
Carry it with mirth;
Lose a realm at pitch-and-toss
Or modestly win the earth.

Jack (*after a pause, sceptically*)
I leave that to the likes of you, sir,
And the likes of Colonel Clive.
I've got enough to do, sir,
Trying to survive.

All John Companee, John Companee,
Comes at first protectively,
Rescues you from tyranny,
One more child sits on the knee
To swell the growing family
Of John Companee.

Dick The bravest of bravest
Of brave men are we.
John, John, John
Companee.

(*Speaking*) So three cheers for the Company. Hip-hip—

Victoria ⎫
                 ⎬ (*together*) Hooray.
Jack   ⎭

Dick And God Save The Queen.

Victoria Thank you. And I hope you will join us in a hymn to the fruits of God's wonderful world. Up on your feet, and sing with me. One-two—
(*Singing*)   Behold the virgin plain,
                                      Behold the fruitful seed

From the back of the audience comes Sally in a white memsahib's dress beating an Indian peasant with a stick

Sally There and there and there and there and how do you like it, eh, you beastly little savage, eh?

Jack runs to stop her, half-way up the aisle, grabs the stick and struggles with her

Jack Sally, Sally, stop it. By God, what's got into you?

Sally I haven't done with him yet.

Jack You've done too bloody much by far. (*To the Indian*) Tikh-hai, Johnny, vamoose, juldi-juldi.

The Indian runs off

Sally tries to grab him again and when Jack holds her wrists, she bites him so that he has to hold her in his arms from behind

Sally Let go of me, Jack Idle. How dare you hold me in such a fashion.

He releases her, sucks his bite. She adjusts her clothing

Most improper.

Jack I beg your pardon but you'd have killed that poor native if I hadn't stopped you.

Sally I wanted to! I wanted to flay his nigger skin till it bled, the same as he did to his poor black bullock.

Jack Oh, is that it? Cruelty to animals?

Sally Have you seen the way they treat their oxen? Seen them flog their starving horses and kick their wretched dogs?

Jack (*breaking the stick she used*) You can't make people live like beasts then expect them to act as saints.

Sally The poor at home don't beat their animals.

Jack Not when you're looking. They think of you as half-way gentry and toffs are known to be as soft on animals as they're hard on people.

Sally Is that *really* how they think of me?

Jack You're the village schoolma'am, Sir Richard's ward—

Sally D'you think that's how *he* sees me?

Jack Who?

Dick This is India, Sally. Their ways aren't ours. We're here to protect them, perhaps to raise them—their only hope is under our protection. And *our* only hope of converting them is gentlemanly example. Two hundred and fifty million of them, a few hundred of us.

Jack If they all spat at once we'd drown.

Dick Firm we must be but merciful.

Sally is crying

Sally I'll go to him. I'll ask forgiveness.

Victoria That would be excessive, child.

Sally What then?

Victoria Some bakshish. A few annas?

Dick nods

Sally And I'll tell him the news.

Dick What's that?

Sally About Jesus. I'll tell them all. I'll start a Bible class, just like at home . . .

She goes after the Indian

Victoria (*following*) We already have one, child.

Victoria exits

Dick She's an enthusiast, our Sally.

Jack She *does* blow hot and cold a bit.

Dick   Yes, first hot then cold
                         Cruel only to be kind
                         That's how to educate the savage mind.
                         So, boys and girls, eyes front and only think
                         The map may turn blood red before it's pink.

Dick and Jack exit

Dodo enters, dressed as a hunting memsahib, sitting on the howdah of a baby elephant. She jumps down and looks about, holding a smoking shotgun. Upward follows, similarly dressed, also with a gun. Bearers and servants enter behind

Dodo Missed him again.

Upward Why don't you let him go, my sweet? He must be the last tiger left in the whole sub-continent.

Dodo Stuff! The place is infested with them. They're a pest.

Upward How about some leopard? The Ganges is teeming with crocodile.

Dodo I think I see him over there, skulking in the brush.

Upward Sorry, madam, I can't keep up with you.

Dodo waves her gun over the stalls. Upward sits, exhausted and hot. He is served with drinks by bearers. Dodo puts her gun down, looks at the elephant who is being fed by servants. She admires the trunk, ogles the audience

Dodo (*going to sit beside him*) *Quelle proboscis! Pas possible!* Why so censorious, *chéri*? You, the mighty hunter! The moment we met you scored a bull's-eye, right in the heart.

Upward My little cherub, I can't make it out. You are in every way all I desire in a lover—

Dodo Tell me, *encore, tout de suite.*

Upward Title, Mistress of Foxhounds, a vast country seat. But why *me*? A mere commoner?

Dodo A *je ne sais quoi.*

Upward The poppy I've got in the bank?

Dodo A *nostalgie de la boue.*

Upward You know I don't parlay the lingo.

Dodo Longing for the mud. *Compris*? Understand?

Upward I'm beginning to.

A waltz has begun, which Dodo sings in the style of a French cabaret song

Dodo Oh thank you.

Music 7: Nostalgie De La Boue

(*Singing*)

> I'm seated in a smart café
> When off the Avenue
> There comes a scent I must obey,
> A fragrance of the zoo—
> Part chimpanzee, part working-man,
> There's nothing I can do
> But follow like a courtesan,
> That's *nostalgie de la boue.*

> The upper set have always made
> Illicit rendezvous
> With what they call "a bit of trade"
> They long for what's taboo
> A Blackamoor, a Roman slave,

It's *chacun à son goût*,
They teach us how to misbehave,
That's *nostalgie de la boue.*

They say Mr Gladstone's particular whim in
The *obscurité de la nuit*
Is to roam about London and save fallen
women—

Upward   D'you think he would save one for *me?*
Dodo   The more *superbe* my own *toilette*
(And this is *entre nous*),
The more I crave the honest sweat
Of such a beast as you ...
When Bonaparte had been away
He'd send a billet-doux:
"Don't wash, I'm coming home today."
That's *nostalgie de la boue. Oui Oui.*
Both   That's *nostalgie de la boue.*

*They waltz about, Dodo swirling till Upward reels dizzily. The elephant joins
in and the chorus. Then a decelerando and she sings con espressione: to the
elephant*

Dodo   My husband was a dunderhead
Beside a man like you,
I've found that when it's time for bed
Best choose a parvenu.
For after all what can be done
With all that noble blood?
A lady can have far more fun
By wallowing in the mud—*compris?*

Both   That's *nostalgie de la boue*—
Upward   Oui, Oui—
All   That's *nostalgie de la boue!*

Dodo and the elephant dance off. Upward follows

SCENE 6

The Opium Auction

*The frontcloth falls, based on contemporary prints of the East India Com-
pany's Calcutta warehouses: cavernous buildings fitted with shelves receding
to the distance and rising to heights well above the proscenium arch, stacked
with balls of drying opium and ladders and catwalks for the workers to reach
them all*

Music 7A: We Sailed Downstream

Clerks We sailed downstream and in the end
Arrived here in Calcutta,
Where most of the Indians seem to spend
Their whole lives in the gutter.
We told one chap, "It isn't nice,
You should be hale and hearty."
He answered, "We can't afford the rice."
So we said, "Then, eat chapatti!"

Victoria When people claim we're trading on men's vices,
The Crown must take an interest in the prices.
Can't miss this opportunity to scan 'um,
This trade brings us one million pounds per annum.

She changes to become the Auctioneer

Auctioneer Good-evening gentlemen and welcome to the East India Company's opium auction. Nice to see the old familiar faces—and one or two new ones to keep us all on our toes. Trade always needs new blood. You know as well as I do that only the finest opium is sold here and that's what the Chinaman wants. So don't look a gift-horse in the mouth, friends. Very well, let's begin. Lot one: ten chests of the finest opium from Patna, each one hundred and forty pounds in weight, who'll start me at four hundred pounds?

Dick Obadiah, who are all these people?

Auctioneer Four hundred pounds.

Upward The private shippers, like myself.

Auctioneer Four hundred and fifty pounds.

Upward The Merchant Venturers who've taken on ourselves——

Auctioneer Five hundred pounds.

Upward —the hazardous task of keeping open the China connection.

Auctioneer Five hundred and fifty pounds for this, the Château-Lafite of poppy, eagerly awaited in Canton and points north?

Upward And if we have a good day's buying——

Auctioneer Six hundred pounds.

Upward —our clipper, *Red Rover*, will ride deep through the Indian Ocean——

Auctioneer Six hundred pounds against you.

Upward —with all we'll have aboard.

Auctioneer Six hundred pounds. I'm going to have to hurry you now, there's a lot to get through. For six hundred pounds then, for the last time, going, going, gone! (*She brings the hammer down*)

Clerk Mister Lancelot Dent of Dent and Davison.

Dick You didn't bid, Obadiah?

Upward Bit too pricey for me, Dick.

Auctioneer Lot two is one dozen chests of second-grade Benares.

Dick Why don't the Company take it to Canton in their own ships?

Auctioneer One hundred and twenty pounds in weight each chest.

Upward Dear boy, the Company is virtually the Crown itself in India. We can't involve it in anything shady.

Dick And is it shady?

Upward Not at all.

Auctioneer An unpretentious but very smokable dope.

Upward The safest and most gentleman-like speculation I am aware of. But it is against the law.

Auctioneer Shall we say three hundred pounds to start.

Dick To take poppy to China?

Upward To import it, yes. The Emperor forbids it.

Auctioneer Come along gentlemen.

Dick But the Chinaman wants it, don't he?

Upward Don't he just! Do you want to bid for this lot?

Dick Yes.

Auctioneer We'll be here till the monsoon season at this rate.

Upward But this old Charlie Chan can control the trade ... or try to.

Auctioneer Who'll start me at three hundred pounds?

Upward If he felt like applying the squeeze, he could cut off the tea supply completely. Three hundred pounds.

Dick Three hundred pounds.

Auctioneer Thank you. At three hundred pounds.

Upward Your English cuppa China tea is what it's all about.

Auctioneer Three hundred and twenty pounds.

Upward The government's tax on tea paid for the war against Boney. Three hundred and forty pounds.

Dick Three hundred and forty pounds.

Auctioneer At three hundred and forty pounds.

Upward So we had to discover something they wanted as much as we wanted their tea.

Auctioneer Against you at three hundred and forty pounds, Mr Matheson.

Dick And that's poppy?

Auctioneer Three hundred and forty pounds once.

Upward I see you're not just a pretty face.

Auctioneer Three hundred and forty pounds twice. You finished Mr Matheson? Are you all done at three hundred and forty pounds for the last time. Going, going, gone to Sir Richard Whittington. Well done, sir. A new partnership joins Dent-Davison and Jardine-Matheson. Upward-Whittington.

Upward Well done, my boy.

Auctioneer Now if you'll follow me, we'll go down the godown for the next lot, a perfectly acceptable smoke ordinaire. ...

He moves on

Dick and Upward take his place onstage. Dick looks at the trunk he's bought

Dick Eight thousand addicts, eh, that chest alone? (*Looking round at the shelves piled high*) So where on earth shall we find customers for all this?

Upward China's population's three hundred and fifty million. And trade's going up by leaps and bounds. We're talking in the region of twenty million customers.

Dick I see what you mean by a safe speculation.

Upward John Chinaman will soon be paying more for his pipe than John Bull pays for his cuppa and we'll have achieved a balance of payments.

Auctioneer (*off*) Going, going, gone!

Upward I wish we were. I'm never sorry to see the last of Calcutta.

He sings to his old refrain: "When I Was a Lad" (Music 7b)

	I met a Yankee face to face,
	Behaving very large
	"You Brits", he said, "Have made this place
	The arsehole of the Raj."
Others	In-fernal cheek! How juvenile!
	Whatever did you do?
Upward	I asked him with a pleasant smile
	"And are you passing through?"
Clerks	Oh that's the way. Yes, that's the style!
	"The shit was passing through!"

They all go, laughing delightedly

SCENE 7

The hold of the "Red Rover"

The maritime music again (Music 7c). Storm, high winds, lightning, thunder

During all this the cloth flies and dim realistic lighting shows the hold of the "Red Rover". Many chests of opium are stacked on shelves but some are on the stage floor. Between them, on a bed of straw, lies Randy with an ice-pack on his head and a large equine thermometer in his mouth. Jack sits beside him on a three-legged stool, holding one fetlock and looking at his fob watch. The music fades away but sounds of creaking timbers continue through this scene

Jack Hallo, cabin boys and girls. Well, old son. (*He takes out and looks at the thermometer*) You must be feeling better? Fancy a bite to eat?

Jack offers a bucket of food but Randy soon gives up. Jack puts the bucket nearby

Perhaps you'd like to hear me sing some tunes
Accompanying myself on spoons?
Thank you, Professor.

Randy shakes his head. Jack shrugs

Still missing Cherry, that's your trouble. Homesick and lovesick and seasick. But one of these days you'll be home again and in clover. You'll be keen enough on your oats then.

Randy nods, whispers in Jack's ear

Me and Sally? I'd like to think so. She's fond of me, all right, like a bosom pal, but I *burn* for her! And d'you know when she kisses me, she rubs her body against mine and bites my ear and tickles my palms and when she sits on my lap she must be able to feel my longing through my corduroys. Does she know what she's doing? I always have to go and have some other girl right after—the village maids at home, the tarts in London, that Indian dancer in Calcutta. Only fourteen but she taught me a few things I'd like to pass on to Sally! (*He moves to whisper in Randy's ear*) But it seems to me she fancies Sir Richard. Her guardian. (*He talks to the audience*) There's something not quite right about him. I only wish I could put my finger on it.

Randy laughs again

Oh, for gawd's sake.

Randy shrugs, hides his face with his hoof. Jack goes on to the audience

But it would be a wonderful match for *her*, I know. Lady Whittington coming down the grand staircase for the finale in a *diamanté* crinoline and Sir Richard in a close-fitting bodice, fish-net tights and high-heeled boots singing that they'll be happy ever after. That's how it should be. To him that hath it shall be given. Whoa.

Dick and Sally come in, staggering

Sally Randy! Up on your feet so soon!

A great swoop of the ship takes all of them staggering about the stage. Randy collapses between the chests. The others in a heap, laughing

Dick Having a good trip? (*He takes a ball of opium*) Strange to imagine the power that's here!
Sally It looks for all the world like putty.
Dick So much healing, so many dreams, such magic!
Jack I'd sooner have reality.
Sally We all need dreams, Jack. Some door in the wall, some way of breathing under water, some paradise where the one you love loves you . . .

Sally looks at Dick, Jack looks at Sally

Dick Of course, it has to be rendered down first. (*He begins unpacking a bag he's brought*)
Jack What's the good if it isn't true?
Dick Refined and simmered till it's pure enough—
Jack You've got to wake up sooner or later—
Sally Later then. Let it be later.
Jack I can't agree.
Sally Most people would.
Dick Right, Sally! Or we should not be sailing with this cargo, for Canton. Embarking on another adventure! Jack, will you join us in the greatest lark of all? (*From the bag he's brought a small box, a bamboo pipe, a box of*

*matches, a spoon-headed needle and is lighting the lamp. He shows a
substance in the box)* This is it—our merchandise, ready for consumption.
I want to be sure we bring a blessing to China, not a curse.

Jack A blessing?

Dick Peace of mind. (*He heats a pellet the size of a pea on the needle*)

Jack My grandpa told me Colonel Clive died of it.

Dick We're always in danger, Jack. Crossing the road we risk our lives.

Jack Danger's not the same as slavery.

Sally Who did most to abolish slavery? William Wilberforce. Took opium
every day for forty years.

Dick There is nothing exotic or Asian about this wonderful consolation;
Jack.

*He puts the pellet of paste into the bowl of the pipe and lights it at the lamp. He
draws on the pipe. Later he passes it to Sally*

Only think what a blessing it must be to the men and women back in
England who mine the coal that feeds the factories!

Sally Or to the children in the mills making the cotton clothes.

Dick That we sell to the peasants in India.

Sally That frees the Indians from their own mills to grow the poppy—

Dick That we sell to China to buy the tea to bring back to Britain—

Sally To quench the thirst of the men and women who mine the coal that
feeds the factories.

Dick Free trade in action, Sally. Let's see if it's the Magic Lamp they claim.

They've all smoked now and continue

*The music swells as the smoke swirls about the stage floor. The Lights change
and a scrim probably comes down for moving films to be shown as part of the
transformation scene which follows*

*The walls of the ship's hold are flown; flying Dancers arrive from above,
over the audience's heads, some rise from traps. The dreamers are lost*

*The Garden of Eden appears, a Douanier Rousseau paradise where animals
appear with humans—elephants, birds, crocodiles, Randy. Dodo and
Upward swing on a great trapeze, make love. Sally in flowing draperies
makes love to Dick and Jack in turn. The animals couple with naked men
and women*

Sally It's magic.

Jack I'm going . . .

Sally I'm going, going, gone . . .

Dick Swallow me, swallow me, swallow me soon . . .

Music 8: Poppy

(See score for counterpoint and chanting)

Poppy,
Whisper of thunder
Roaring of dove,
Bright sky that's under
Valleys above.

Poppy,
Empress of flowers
Burnt by the Moon,
Use all your powers:
Swallow me soon.

How can I ever escape from the spell
Of towering oceans heard in a shell?
Or flying with tigers half through the night,
Cascading down forests of submarine light?

Warm-blooded geckoes
Pricking their ears,
Catching the echoes
Of future years.
Poppy!

Victoria appears, robed and crowned, and from the other side Prince Albert, equally grand. The Emperor of China, above, seems to officiate at their wedding. As they approach, he makes a sign and both are stripped. Everyone gazes at their nakedness. No pain in any of this, only gratification, sheer pleasure

The Lights finally go as the music dies. Then Lights come up on an interval front-cloth advertising several of the popular opiates of the time: Mother Bailey's Quieting Syrup, Godfrey's Cordial, Mrs Winslow's Sedative Solution, Dr Collis-Browne's Chlorodine . . .

House Lights up. The cloth, of course, remains to be read

ACT II

Scene 1 (Prologue)

Victoria is being dressed for her wedding by ladies-in-waiting. They sing

Music 9: Bounty of the Earth

British
Rejoice! For Harvest Home.
Oh, see the generous crops!
From limits far as man can roam
Replenishing the shops.
Grateful retailers
Calculate its worth
How can it fail us?
The Bounty of the Earth.
Amen.

A change to gongs and exotic harmonies brings on the Emperor, still on high but lower now

Emperor Greetings, wild and distant chieftainess!

Victoria How nice you thought of dropping in, Your Highness—
A chance for you to see my wedding dress.
White satin trimmed with finest English lace.

Emperor Felicitations.

Victoria Help my ignorance—have you an empress?

Emperor Eight queens first class. Ninety concubines.

Victoria There are no concubines among my subjects.

Emperor None? Your Prince—

Victoria Prince Albert—

Emperor Yes. Has none? I almost envy him. So restful.

Victoria The missionaries would, I'm sure, be happy to explain our Lord's teaching on this and—

Emperor Is that the same lord that was slowly tortured to death while his father watched and gave no help? And now does he grudge us the joys of love but smiles at the sale of Foreign Shit?

Victoria makes to go. The Emperor throws a flash bomb

This trade must cease. Have the plant plucked up. Grow rice instead. Tremblingly obey!

Victoria My government will not submit to any limitation.
The bounty of the earth is to be shared by every nation.

Victoria and Ladies
Rejoice! For Harvest Home.
Oh, see the generous crops!
From the limit far as man can roam
Replenishing the shops.

Grateful retailers
Calculate its worth

How can it fail us?

The Bounty of the Earth
Amen.

Mandarins
A home that isn't yours.
Poisoned Poppy.
The wealth of India—loads of
   shit
Imported by your ships,
All for profit.
Evil Barbarian!
That's enough——
High time you made kow-tow,
Young Queen,
Or all too soon you will find
What it can mean
To provoke the Imperial rage.

Victoria and the Ladies exit

The Emperor tries a conjuring trick or two. He fails one, tries again. He throws down his props in anger

Lin approaches, doing kowtow. He is forty, handome. In this scene he is humble

Lin Commissioner Lin Tse-tsii!
Emperor Go south to Canton. The hour has come to purge the bowel of Kwangtung Province. A bird tells me our Viceroy there is crooked as the small intestine. His court blighted with corruption. Take care you don't believe his honeyed words.
Lin I fly to my commission like a hawk, sped by the breeze of your sublime favour. I'll cure Canton's corruption with a thousand cuts. Heads will roll, the Foreign Shit will burn.
Emperor I only wish it weren't too late to save my son.
Lin How is the heir apparent?
Emperor Stupefied. With black receding gums. The best the poppy can do is kill him. The corridors of paradise are clouded by the smoke. He and his friends have each a Foreign Devil on their backs. Our only hope now is he dies before me or you will have an Emperor who chases the dragon day and night.
Lin The savages shall be sent home, have no fear.
Emperor Take this ring as sign of our commission. Touch it when there's trouble. It may help.
Lin (*receiving the ring and kissing it*) I shall, My Emperor.
Emperor   Go now and smack these brats till they start weeping
                New broom by my command, begin your sweeping.

The Emperor vanishes

Lin turns and walks swiftly into the next scene

SCENE 2

Canton

Lin I'll be a broom all right, I'll be a scourge. I'll cauterize corruption in Canton. But that won't save the Manchu Dynasty.

Mandarins   The Emperor confounds all natural law:
                 Sunlight shines upon us from the north.

Lin Glorious Rectitude is concerned about the Canton Port Authority. This province is most known for smoking poppy.

Mandarin We regularly strangle those we catch.

Lin From now on those who've got the habit shall be cured. Strangling and beheading will be saved for those officials who take bribes. And those commanders who give chase too late to catch the smugglers' ships. And we must also purge the Foreign Devils of their shit as rhubarb cured their constipation.

Mandarins (*aside*) But that won't save the Manchu Dynasty.

Mandarin 1 A delegation of Fanqui barbarians grovel even now for an audience.

Lin What land are they from?

Mandarin 1 Who can tell?

Mandarin 2 They are Fanqui.

Music 10: They All Look the Same to Us

Lin	We describe all savages as Fanquis But there are innumberable races— English, Spanners, Turkey, Frenchie, Yankees, Coming from as many different places.
Chorus	They all look the same to us Scarlet face and yellow hair, Noses too conspicuous, Eyes that permanently stare. In a word they're barbarous And they look the same to us.
Girls	With their tied-up legs they walk Gracefully as buffalo,
Boys	Through their broken teeth they talk Silver-tongued as any crow.
All	Sounding all the same to us.

	When they eat they wage a kind of battle.
	    (Whatever for?)
	Using swords to tear their food apart. (Are you
	    sure?)
	Hacking bits off carcasses of cattle. (Say no
	    more!)
	Understandably this makes them fart.

Gluttonous, omnivorous,
Lecherous and murderous,
Verminous, villainous,
Voracious and vainglorious.

It's not racial prejudice
For since the day they came to us
It's stood up to analysis
Methodical and rigorous
That they all look the same,
They all look the same,
Every Fanqui
English, French or Yankee
Look the same to us.

Lin If the Fanqui have grovelled long enough let them in.

Dick, Upward and Dodo enter to a brazen march

Upward Hallo, Number One Boss Man. My Missie Upside, Number One Shopman Blitish side. Plenty contentee come see you. Plentee long time my wishee look see you. All same Number Two Mandarins they say "Tomollo, tomollo". Me say them, "Tomollo him never come". Savvy?
Lin Number One Shopman plentee too much hullee. Tomollo come bimeby. Me come Peking chop-chop, want plenty why-how-where.
Upward S'welp me bob, this geezer's from His Nibs.
Lin Big Boss Number One no contentee. Now me catchee monkey.
Upward Dear oh dear. Plis, say hallo Number Two Shopman. Missee Dick Rittington.
Dick Your servant, sir.
Upward Speak pidgin. All they understand.
Dick Me Missee Dick.
Lin They seem to think this creature is a man.
Dick (*impatiently*) Plis, say hallo Mummy Number Two Shopman.

Dodo curtsies, nearly topples

Dodo Ooops. Velly solly. Long time no curtsy.
Lin Savvy no can. Your say so? This Mummy?
Dodo Yes, that's me. *Moi*!
Lin No women ever looked or sounded so. Not even a barbarian.

The Mandarins laugh

Dodo I don't wonder you laugh. This great boy really is my Dick.
Dick Speak pidgin.
Dodo No. We understand each other. He can't believe I'm such a big boy's mother.
Lin To business now. Harkee Missee Upside, Missee Dick. You send petition Number One, he no like. Tao-Kuang Son of Heaven he say No Can Do. Look see letter. (*He reads from a scroll*) Item One: Incomparable

Climax now decrees all Fanqui never more pollute the Celestial Kingdom with Foreign Shit.

Dick Hells bells!

Lin Item Two: Out of compassion we shall continue providing you with tea you need and the silk and the cinnamon—and of course the rhubarb, without which, as we know, you would all die.

Upward Rhubarb?

Dick Rhubarb?

Dodo Rhubarb?

Upward Rhubarb?

Dick Rhubarb?

Dodo Rhubarb?

Lin Item Three: As earnest of your good intent, all your stocks of opium shall now be given up as contraband.

Upward He's joking.

Dick I fear not.

Lin Not one cattie, not one chest of this pernicious poison must remain.

Dick Our poppy poisonous? The best Benares.

Lin And all this must be done within a week!

Dick (*stepping forward*) Number One no can do!

Gongs. Swords. Guards. The Chinese all stand

Lin Do not incur the Son of Heaven's wrath!

Dick I am but an Englishman. We've beaten Bonaparte by land and sea—

Upward Sir Richard, hold your horses—

Dodo Let him speak.

Dick We rule the waves, our empire spans the globe, Britain is the workshop of the world—

As Dick speaks, Lin gestures to the Guards who now take hold of the British. There's a struggle and the British fight. Lin steps downstage, rubs the ring on his finger

Music, thunder, the Emperor appears above, perhaps in a film with hugely amplified voice

The Chinese throw themselves on the ground, the British cower

Emperor No more! Surrender the Foreign Shit! This is the command of the Son of Heaven. Grovel hereat. Slavishly cringe and tremble at the knee. These words are inscribed with the Vermilion Pencil.

More noise, thunder, lightning, music. The British are swept from the stage by Soldiers. Everyone is whirled away as if by a cyclone . . .

. . . Leaving only Lin, prostrate upon the stage before the Emperor's image, which now fades to be replaced by the Emperor himself, smaller and human-looking, coughing slightly

Emperor Get up, Lin. We are alone.

Lin (*rising*) I thank you, Majesty.

Emperor   Such gestures aren't to be relied upon.
                 With every passing year my magic fails.
                 I sometimes find there's nothing up my sleeve.

He collapses wearily on one of the thrones

Lin   I feel your power strengthen my resolve.
Emperor   Don't go too far, that's all I ask.
                 The savages are strong.
Lin   Our fleet of fireships only need appear
                 To fill their savage hearts with abject fear.
                 Next our cannon carved with lions' heads will roar.
Emperor   All very well. What if they come ashore?
Lin   No chance. On land they roll like buffalo.
                 They've use of neither fist nor sword nor bow.
                 I'm confident of their complete defeat
                 On land. But they won't ever pass our fleet.
Emperor   Wash my kingdom clear of shit and you shall be my
                 Viceroy of Kiangsu.
Lin (*bowing*) I'll save Canton and that will save Kwantung.
Emperor I only wish you could save my son.

He claps his hands and vanishes

Lin   Too late for him, soft fruit of blighted tree.
                 Perhaps too late for you.
                 And certainly, no matter what I do,
                 Far too late for the Manchu Dynasty.

He takes a striker, wields it like a sword and strikes the gong

SCENE 3

Jack, Sally, and Dick

A reprise of "Whoa, Boy" from the orchestra (Music 10G)

Frontcloth: before the factories on the waterfront at Canton: elegant houses with flags of various nations flying above, Union Jack centre

Jack enters with Randy, strapped to a cart piled with laundry bags. Centre, some fall off, Jack shouts "Whoa, Boy" and sings a few phrases of the song. He replaces the bags

Jack Hallo Chinese boys and girls. Fetch this, carry that! You'd think old Lady Dildo would have enough coolies to do her dirty work, but no, there's always some left over for us, ain't there, son?

Randy nods his head

"Idle, get my linen back from Wishee-Washee and Idle, when you've done that, run down the off-licence for some crisps and a couple of quarts of rice-wine." (*He finishes, mopping his brow and sits on the cart*)

Well, now at last we've shook off the old Gorgon
It's time to play for you on my mouth-organ.

Thank you, Professor.

He takes it out, signals the professor, who starts an intro but . . .

Sally enters, unseen by Jack, radiantly happy, in white with a parasol. She gestures to the audience for silence and puts her hands over Jack's eyes

Music continues throughout, a reprise of "Whoa, boy"

If I guess who it is, shall I get a kiss?
Sally Jack really! Don't you think of anything else?
Jack Most of the time I've got to, but when I get a moment to myself—
Sally You must try, really! Look about you—at wonderful Canton, the busy riverside with its teeming life, the quaint trading factories where all us Europeans live—
Jack Well, as I say, I don't get that much time—
Sally Well, nor do I. What with the dinners and musical evenings and fancy-dress balls. Above all, the river! With all the hundreds of different craft plying up and down. Have you seen those beautiful flower-ships?
Jack (*shocked*) Eh?
Sally Don't you think they're pretty?
Jack If you like that sort of thing, yes.
Sally Do you know what Lady Dodo told me?
Jack What?
Sally Those aren't flower-*ships* at all.
Jack Go on.
Sally They're floating houses of ill-repute.
Jack Get out!

Randy laughs, Jack smacks him

Sally One day soon, Jack, I want you to take me on one of those vessels.
Jack You do?
Sally Wouldn't you like to?
Jack Just you and me?
Sally And the flower-girls, yes.
Jack Whoa, boy steady. What are you suggesting?
Sally What d'you think? To start a Bible class, of course.
Jack How are they going to read the Bible?
Sally Oh, I've done some of the most important bits in to pidgin. The twenty-third psalm, for instance: "Number One Sheep Boss, him belong me. Me muchee contentee."

They laugh

But I'm learning Cantonese as well. Then I'll really be able to serve Dick

Jack   Whoa, Sal,
                 No, Sal,
                 Slow, Sal.

Both   'Cos all that wild fluctuation
                 In your circulation
                 Is a clear indication
                 How much you care.

                 So whoa, there.

Dick enters

Dick What's this damned hullabaloo?

They stop but the band continues

(*To the band*) Stop your blasted row, do you hear me?

They all do, surprised. Silence. Dick's angry

Where d'you think you are? Not in the back streets of Wapping now. We
have an example to set to all the other merchants. Krauts and Dagoes
everywhere. Not to mention the Chinks.

Sally We were only singing a reprise of our Act One duet—
Dick Be quiet, Sally, I'm speaking to Idle here.
Sally Idle?

Jack, loading the bags, pauses and looks at him

Dick Get that linen to the laundry and look sharp about it.
Jack I think I've given you no occasion to complain of my——
Dick Don't answer back. I've had too much of your confounded lip.

He turns away as Jack loads. Randy noses Dick's behind

And take that mangy beast away, out of my sight. He stinks to heaven.
Jack Right. (*He finishes loading, starts to lead Randy off*)
Dick Right who?
Jack (*after a pause, ironically touching his forelock*) Squire.

Jack goes off with Randy

Sally (*after he's gone*) Dick, I beg your pardon if I led Jack into a harmless
frolic that——
Dick Sally, as your guardian, I instruct you now to see less of him. I'm sure
he's a good fellow at heart but he's a damned sight too familiar. That old
lackadaisical attitude's not good enough for the new age we live in now.
He must learn to pull his socks up, stir his stumps, get on his rickshaw.
Sally Is it right to regard Jack so because he's only a servant? Didn't Our
Lord teach us to break down the barriers of caste and class?
Dick But He didn't have to deal with some of the elements we've got today.
A lot of ruffians who'd give working men a voice in Parliament? Jack Idle
a vote? You don't think Our Lord would have drunk to that?

Sally A cat may look at a king. Why shouldn't a manservant talk to a village schoolma'am?

Dick Or the schoolma'am to the squire? The orphan girl to the knight? Is that what you mean?

He takes her hands, kisses them, she's confused

Dear sweet village lass. As pure as an English summer's day.

Sally suddenly kisses Dick on the lips, pressing herself against him. He recoils and holds her at arm's length

Sally, what are you doing, child?

Sally I love you. I couldn't help myself.

Dick All right, Sally. I understand but,

Music 10H: Whoa Boy *(Reprise)*

When that sort of hunger surges,
Think; new age need new urges:
Sublimate your appetites,
Emulate hermaphrodites.
Stricken with a low desire,
Try to think of something higher,
Intellectual intercourse is
Much the best so hold your horses.

Dick smiles and exits jauntily

Sally

So however it's hurting
Hide it from view
Till the moment you're certain
That the raging desire
That's got you on fire
Is burning him too.

One day
We may
Horse-play.
Birds sing;
Gold ring.
Offspring

But till we walk down the aisle
We must try self-denial
With a brave little smile
Upon our faces—

She drinks from her laudanum flask

No, Sal,
Slow, gal . . . .

She exits

SCENE 4

Inside the factories

The cloth flies to show the inside of the factories: Upward's office, a Cantonese version of the London one: same chandeliers, same four Clerks, now in linen, Chinese Servants fan them. The Clerks sing a reprise of their opening song

Music: In These Chambers *(Reprise)*

Clerks   In this climate hot and sticky
                              Long way from our bailiwickee
                              Obadiah and Sir Dickee
                              Keepee moving upside.

                              Bureaucratic interference
                              May require a little clearance
                              But upon its disappearance

                              We'll see profits mounting higher
                              Giving us our heart's desire—
                              Back to England, soon retire—
                              Bless you, Obadiah!

Upward has entered, asked applause for chandeliers. Dick follows, agitated

Song: When I Was a Boy *(Reprise)*

Dick   We obviously don't agree
                              About this situation.
                              That mandarin, it seems to me,
                              Is all for confiscation.
Upward   But anyone who knows the East
                              Will you see this gesture's formal.
                              When all the important palms are greased
                              We'll carry on as normal.

The music ends

Dick And what if we take a moral stand?
Upward Dick, this isn't Cheapside, this is China.
Dick Then we must raise China's morals till they are level with Cheapside's. However—such a crisis as this certainly means I must cancel my trading mission up the coast.
Upward Say not so, my boy. We depend on your expedition. The market's dull, trade's sluggish. The harvest in India was so bountiful—thank God—that we've a glut in the hulks. We've nowhere to store it. We need new customers, Dick, fresh trading bases.
Dick Very well, but I wish our crew had a Chinese speaker.

Sally enters, still with a glass of laudanum, from which she sips

Sally Dick, I've found you an interpreter.

Dick The devil you have! Show him in.
Sally Not him. A lady.
Dick A lady?
Sally Miss Fortune. You remember her from India. She's my teacher. I too am learning the local lingo.
Dick Then you could come as well? Is it proper, Obadiah?
Sally Once you've met her, you'll know it's proper. (*She calls off*) Miss Fortune, please come in.
Upward Where is she from?
Sally Nowhere special. She seems to pop up everywhere.

Victoria has come up from a trap in the office, though nobody sees but us. She's dressed as a missionary in black, with a bonnet and umbrella

Victoria Good-afternoon.
Upward (*turning, startled*) Excuse me, ma'am, I never heard the door.
Victoria All doors are open to the word of God.
Upward Jesus. I don't like this at all. I trust I'm as good a Christian as the next man but in our trade religious scruples can be a royal pain in the arse.

Victoria fans herself vigorously, not amused

If you'll excuse the expression, ma'am.
Dick There are *two* ladies present sir.
Upward What? Oh, yes, sorry, lass.
Sally (*to Dick, entranced*) Please don't think of it.
Upward But I still don't like it.
Sally
Victoria } (*together*) Why ever not?

Music 12: The Blessed Trinity

Upward (*speaking*)	Well, madam, I think it's only fair to say This voyage is for stimulating trade.
Dick (*speaking*)	Business is our business, yes, Though we're Christians to a man.
Upward (*speaking*)	Now one of my captains said, "That's fine, Just the kind of voyage I enjoy" — Yet the very first Sunday we put ashore He refused to unload a chest.
Dick (*singing*)	Said he wouldn't do it on the Sabbath Day For Sunday belongs to the Lord.
Upward	Well, I had to relieve him of his command As soon as we regained port. I told him he might be better off with a firm That dealt with tea If he couldn't reconcile commerce with Christianity.
Victoria	But civilization, commerce and Christianity, All go together and all begin with C.

	Four hundred million to be baptized,
	Commercialized and civilized.
	How can this be realized?
	With the blessed trinity!
Dick	I'm not quite sure you understand
	That we shall be smuggling contraband.
Victoria	And Sally and I will be smuggling in
	The blessed word of the Lord,
	Like Peter,
Sally	And Paul;
Victoria	And all the saints
Victoria	And every missionary
Sally	Who's a member of the British and Foreign
	Bible Society.
Victoria	So,
All	Civilization, commerce and Christianity
	All go together and all begin with C.
Victoria	Got to deliver that heathen horde
	So come on, children get aboard
All 4	The ship that's chartered by the Lord;
	That's the blessed trinity.
Upward	Will you tell us, even on the Sabbath Day,
	Are we going to be forced to stop?
Victoria	No, sir, we'll carry on the Lord's business
	A-gathering in the crop.
Upward *(speaking)*	The Lord's I know, but what about mine?
Victoria	I believe they're intertwined.
Upward	You'll interpret the pagan lingo?
Victoria	Yes.
Dick	You'll sell our merchandise?
Victoria	Certainly.
Dick	Will you help take orders?
Upward	Negotiate bribes?
Dick	Arrange concessions?
Upward	And haggle over deals?
Victoria	As long as no-one hinders us
Sally	When we're haggling over souls.
Dick	Lord forbid—
Upward	And s'welp me bob!
Upward ⎱	That's a matter of urgency
Dick ⎰	
All	To bring that race within the embrace of the
	Limited company of
	Civilization, commerce and Christianity—
	All go together and all begin with C.
Victoria	Gonna be gathering dividends
	Like a joyful host of inscrutable friends,
All	Safe in the security of the blessed trinity.

That's civilization, commerce and Christianity,
Gotta be grand in the promised land in such a
          company.

Victoria We're taking off on a heavenly trip
So weigh the anchor, let her rip,

All All aboard the fellowship of the blessed trinity

That's civilization, commerce and Christianity,
Wanna tie all you children with the bonds that
          set you free.
Turn all your capital into prayers,
You could be four hundred millionnaires,
Loaded down with stocks and shares
Of the blessed trinity.

That's civilization, commerce and Christianity,
All go together and all begin with C.
Four hundred million to be baptized,
Commercialized and civilized.
How can this be realized?
With the blessed, the blessed, the blessed,
          blessed
                    trinity
The blessed trinity. C.C.C.

Victoria A compound interest will there be

All Yeah.

Victoria A common wealth of L.S.D.—Oh yeah.

All Oh yeah!

Victoria From civilization, commerce and Christianity,

Dick

Sally From civilization, commerce and Christianity,

Upward

All From civilization, commerce and Christianity,
All go together and all begin with C.
Got to deliver that heathen horde,
So come on children, get on board,
The ship that's chartered by the Lord:
That's the blessed, the blessed, the blessed,
          blessed
                    trinity
The blessed trinity.
C.C.C.

SCENE 5

Canton Palace

Lin enters

Chinese percussion

Lin Full seven times the hour of the monkey has passed by gibbering and exposing itself and still no shit's been handed over by the Foreign Devils. Several wealthy members of the Canton Chamber of Commerce have been strangled in public to encourage the others. But yet the Fanqui haven't sent a pipeful. I am giving them one more day's grace because this is the day they set aside to praise their heathen gods. It behoves us to observe the Confucian maxim regarding hospitality. But when the hour of the dog comes scampering and looking for a tree, I'll blockade the factories. No food, no ships allowed to land, none of our people serving them on pain of death. Tomorrow a few more merchants' heads will be cut off and stuck on poles. I may even prohibit their rhubarb to concentrate the Fanquis' minds.

No matter, I am confident starvation
Will wear them down as soon as constipation

Lin exits

SCENE 6

Outside the factory

A green before the factories. At the back a high wall with a sky cyclorama beyond and some distant pagodas; at one side the waterfront, shown by the rigging of ships; at the other, the façades of the factories at an angle. Standing clear, a flagpole with the British flag fluttering merrily; on the green a garden seat

Randy comes on drawing a cart, now loaded with bundles of bibles and hymn-books, tied with string. He sits wearily and they slide off on to the ground as Jack follows, carrying an armful of bibles. He drops them into the cart

Jack Hallo, Cantonese boys and girls. Don't give in now, Randy. This is the last load.

Randy struggles to his hooves. Jack loads the Bibles

I reckon that clipper would keel over from the weight of Bibles if there wasn't so much opium below to give it ballast. (*He moves downstage, mops his brow with a handkerchief*)

Randy, do you realize it's been a
Long time since I played my ocarina?

Thank you, Professor.

The band starts the intro as Jack tunes up. There is a cry from the Chinese off-stage, beating of gongs, general palaver. Jack looks about, the band falters

Above the wall at the back a severed Chinese head is raised on a pole, dripping blood

Jack doesn't see

> Some barmy Chinese rave-up. The Day of the One-Eared Sloth or something. Take no notice. Maestro!

Randy looks up, sees it, his front part jumps up on his back legs. Jack turns as . . .

The head disappears below

> Did you see something, Randy?

Randy nods, points to the wall. Jack turns back to the audience

> Did *you* see anything, boys and girls? Well, will you promise to tell us if you do? Will you shout out "Behind you". Will you? Thank you, boys and girls (*He starts to play again*)

> *Dick comes from the waterfront*

Dick Come on, Idle, damn you. Get this stuff aboard. We're about to cast off. (*He smacks Randy's haunch*)

> *Randy runs off to the waterfront, pulling the cart*

Jack (*putting away his ocarina*) Ay-Ay, skipper.

> *Jack touches his forelock and follows Randy*

Dick I can't leave him alone for a moment before he's downed tools and started acting the goat. (*To the audience*) And I'll thank you not to lead him on.

> *The male Clerks come from the factory bringing more Bibles, female luggage, etc., followed by Victoria and Sally*

Victoria Mind how you go with those bibles! And that chest is full of medicines for the little heathens, so take care.

> *She follows them off to the waterfront*

Dick Well, Sally, here we are again, bound for another adventure.

> *They come to the front, his arm round her*

Sally I believe I'm the happiest principal girl in the world.

> *Dodo enters from the factories, unseen. She tells us to shush and listens*

Dick Are you not afraid of anything?
Sally Not with you beside me.
Dodo (*aside*) Ay-ay.
Sally And my medicine to keep me calm.

Dick Medicine?

Sally Laudanum.

Dick Ah!

Dodo Hallo, you two! All ready? Oh, I wish I was coming with you. I hear there's excellent shooting up country and I haven't killed a thing for weeks.

Dick Then do, Mother. I have an uneasy feeling matters here are coming to a head.

Cacophony off. The head appears again

Dodo I can't possibly come and I can't leave Obadiah on his own. Who would dust his ornaments?

The head is shown again with the usual clamour. They look round as the head goes

And besides, if there's going to be any trouble, my place is by his side. I'm sure you understand, don't you, Sally?

Sally Oh, yes, I do.

Dodo (*to us*) Ay-ay!

Dick Very well. Let's aboard then if we want to make Macao and the open sea by Wednesday. Be ready, Sally, when I come.

Sally Come when you like, Dick, I'll be ready.

Dodo (*to us*) All together now—ay-ay!

Dick goes to the factories

The Clerks return, crossing

Dodo sits on the bench, confides to the audience

> It takes one girl in love to spot another.
> The time has come for me to act her mother.

Sally, my dear, come and sit by me a minute.

Sally sips from her bottle, sits. Dodo puts her arm round her

The orchestra plays an English folk-tune while she speaks

D'you remember when you and Dick were so high, I used to tell you stories?

Sally I still remember them. I tell them to the village children in school.

Dodo Well, there is one I never told you. Perhaps I should have done but you might not have understood it then. It's about old Sir Richard, Dick's dad. It's strictly for adults only. Now, are you sitting comfortably? Then I'll begin.

Music 13: Sir Richard's Song

(*Singing*)
> Sir Richard was a country squire
> Who looked good on a horse;
> He owned a lot of Worcestershire
> But he hadn't got much sauce.

"You need an heir," his mother said,
"But not off the old block:
The Whittingtons are interbred,
It's time we found new stock."

She dared not trust too much on
Sir Richard's potency,
So dormant was his scutcheon,
So limp his family tree.

With a fol-de-rol and riddle-me-ree,
Come and sing along a song with me.

Sally repeats

Sally   With a fol-de-rol and riddle-me-ree
                   Come and sing along a song with me.
Dodo   There came a charming *arriviste*
                   With beauty, brains and taste;
                   The squire became a ravening beast
                   And married her in haste.
Sally   (*stirring*) Not you?
Dodo   *Oui, moi!*
                   Yes, I was a village girl, my dear,
                   Sir Richard's pride and joy,
                   I set his heart in a whirl, my dear,
                   And gave him a bouncing boy.

                   Alas, he soon stopped caring
                   For me, his better half;
                   And his armoral bearing
                   Was flourished at the staff.

All   With a fol-de-rol
                   And a knicker-knacker-noo,
                   Come and sing along a song, please do.

Sally   With a fol-de-rol
                   And a knicker-knacker-noo
                   Come and sing along a song, please do.

Dodo   He loved to turn the maidens' heads,
                   The maidenheads so pure;
                   While they were making up the beds
                   He'd claim droit de seigneur.

                   He caught one lass and taught her
                   The way to play the game.
                   The hussy had a daughter
                   And Sally was her name.

                   So now your dear half-brother
                   Your guardian has become—

Sally (*staring at her*) You're lying!
Dodo   With a fol-de-rol
                             And a riddle-re-me
                             Come and——
Sally No! It isn't true.
Dodo I told you you hadn't heard that one. But felt it was time you did.
  Before you started——
Sally I don't believe you!

  Jack enters

Jack Come on, Sal, Miss Fortune's asking where you are.

Chinese clamour. Two heads raised on poles, dripping blood

Jack's looking away. He turns to see the heads

Sally (*to Dodo*) You want to put me off so he can marry money.
Dodo A true story. No fairy tale.
Jack Quick, Sally, get aboard. (*He urges her to go*)
Sally Let me alone.
Jack (*touching her arm*) Come on, love, you can't——
Sally (*screaming*) Don't touch me!

  Dick and Upward come from the factories

Dick Ship's company all present and correct. Goodbye, Mother.
Dodo A safe and prosperous mission, son.

*Dick takes a sealed letter, crosses to Sally, who is swigging freely from her
bottle*

Dick Ready, Sally? The tide's waiting.
Sally I'm not going.

Jack shows the heads to Upward

  Victoria returns from the ship

Victoria Come along Sally. I've called all hands on deck to ask God's
  blessing on our enterprise.
Sally (*to her*) I'm staying here.
Victoria And leaving me the only woman? Stuff!
Dick Remember what we said just now, Sal, a new adventure we can share.
Dodo A slight suspicion of the vapours. Her time of month.
Dick Come on everyone, all aboard.

Clamour again. Another head. A ship's bell is heard

  Dick, Sally and Victoria are bustled off by Jack

Dodo waves, remaining

Dodo *Bon voyage*! *Au'voir*! Toodle-oo! See you on the ice. If you can't be
  good be careful. Bye-bye.
Heads on wall Bye-bye!

Laughter. Dodo angrily searches for a missile. She finds a chest marked "SAMPLES" and opens it, takes out small balls of opium about the size of cricket balls, begins throwing them at the heads, as at a coconut shy, so that they hit the sky-cloth behind. Three of the heads drop out of sight and three others are hoisted high on poles. Missiles begin to come from over the wall—apples, oranges, cabbages. Dodo goes on shying over the samples. Chinese clamour and cymbals. Ship's bell and whistle. One of the severed heads comes over. She catches it getting her apron bloody

Music 13: Sir Richard's Song *(Reprise)*

Dodo

Well, after this that bounder Lin
Threw his weight about.
The coolies weren't permitted in
And we could not go out.

But by begging and beseeching we
Were adequately fed
Till one day after retching we
Found arsenic in the bread.

Well, it caused us some disquiet—
We were lucky it was found.
So we all went on a diet
Of whatever grew around.

There was rhubarb in the morning,
There was rhubarb pie at one,
There was rhubarb stew for supper and—

(Speaking)   Excuse me, I must run.

Dodo exits

Scene 7

Outside the factory. Later

Tabs rise on the factory green (as for Scene 6). It is nearing sunset

Jack enters, leading Randy by a carrot on a stick. He allows him to take and eat it greedily

Jack Hungry? Aren't we all? Hallo starving boys and girls. Make the most of it. That's all the supper there is. No more. It's emergency rations from now on.

Randy sits, yawns. Jack looks into the lights

The sun is setting and the time is nigh
For me to sing my favourite lullaby.
Thank you Professor.

Randy lies on the stage, his head in Jack's lap. Jack sings an Albert Chevalier coster song

Music 14: Rock-a-Bye, Randy

(*Singing*)   You're a dear old moke
                And it makes me choke
                When I think of everything that we've been
                        through,
                From the cheery shock,
                My dear old cock,
                As I first set eyes on you.

                Rock-a-bye, Randy, time for a nap;
                Off to the land of nod.
                Oftentimes you have been a blessing, old chap,
                Others a randy old sod.

                We've had our ups and downs, I know,
                I've taken you in hand.
                You liked to come when I said "Go"
                And sit when I said "Stand".

                You've grown on me, tell you straight,
                Right from the start
                But me and my old mate shall never part
                So rock-a-bye, Randy,
                Go to sleep, Randy,
                Randy, rock-a-bye.

Jack looks at Randy's closed eyes. The music continues

(*Speaking*) That's the style, go sleepy-byes and dream of Cherry frisking in an English meadow. And I'll console myself with thoughts of Sally. Where is she now, I wonder? More than a month since she sailed away. Don't ask me what it's all about. (*While talking, he has taken out a pistol. He checks it, removes the catch, looks again at Randy's sleeping head*) This isn't my idea, you know that. But I said if someone's got to do it, *I* must. Anything else would be like sending you off to the knacker's yard—and that's what I saved you from.

He puts the gun at Randy's head. Seconds pass. He cannot pull the trigger. Randy sleeps on the ground, stirring slightly

    The Clerks enter

But Christ, why should I? What's it for?
1st Clerk Food's scarce, Jack.
2nd Clerk It's us or them. Come on.

Jack shoots him and Randy drops dead

    They cart off Randy's corpse

The lullaby is resumed

Jack   Remember your old pal sometime
                          When you're up above
                          In painted fields of pantomime,
                          Grazing with your love.
                          So rock-a-bye, Randy ...
                          Go to sleep, Randy

He gives up and exits

Music plays out in orchestra

SCENE 8

The same. Morning

Bright morning light. Half a dozen Chinese heads on poles beyond the wall. The flag's missing from the pole

Dodo comes on with the flag and fastens it to the rope

Drums behind the wall and another head joins the others

Dodo (*seeing it*) Top of the morning to you.

Upward comes on from the waterfront

Upward Oh, my dear, you're up with the lark.
Dodo I've been washing the flag after what they threw at it yesterday.
Upward Did they?
Dodo Did they not! Tarred it with turd and marred it with *merde*.
Upward Talk about Hoo Flung Dung!

She hoists the flag while Upward sits on the bench. The flag flutters

Dodo And where have you been so early?
Upward I've made arrangements to hand over all our stocks of poppy, you'll be happy to hear.
Dodo Happy to hear? Happy to hear? I'm not happy to hear it at all. I'm *désolée*. You mean to say you've given in?
Upward Given in? I wouldn't say that.
Dodo Well, I would. I say it as a mere woman. And Dick would too if he wasn't in Ting-Hai with the Task Force. It's cowardice.
Upward No, my sugar. Calculation. Last night a note was smuggled up river from Macao—an undertaking that, should we be compelled to surrender our merchandise to the Chinks, Her Majesty's Government will indemnify us for every chest.
Dodo Are you saying the British taxpayer will foot the bill for all our poppy?
Upward I do, my dear. And if old Fu Manchu destroys it all, as he intends,

he will turn a glut into a shortage. A poppy mountain into a dearth. What do you think will happen then?

Dodo The price goes up?

Upward My clippers are already at sea with the fresh crop from India. And, if Dick's been lucky up the coast, the demands will push the price sky-high.

Dodo So we can't lose either way.

Upward And we may win twice—once from the Chinese hopheads.

Dodo Once from the British tax-payer. My bull!

She embraces him, he is crushed

Upward My bear.

Smoke has been drifting across the stage from the factories

Upward Is something burning?

Dodo I hope it isn't breakfast.

Upward Breakfast? I'm starving after all that jaw.

Dodo I'm glad because there's a special treat. A nice rump steak.

Upward The devil there is! A real beef steak?

Dodo (*winking at the audience*) Well, almost.

Upward Marvellous! I could eat a horse.

   He follows Dodo off

The Frontcloth comes down as Chinese music is played

SCENE 9

Battle of Ting-Hai

Smoke continues to drift across

Lin enters. He clears a breathing space with his fan

Lin No need for alarm. That's not Canton that's burning but the Foreign Shit. All is collected. Twenty thousand chests. We think the burning will take twenty days. We've sung already to the goddess of the sky asking for forgiveness for polluting her domain.

Flute and percussion. He takes up another posture

The Emperor has sent a gift of roebuck flesh, which signifies "promotion is assured". As soon as the trafficking in Shit has stopped, I'll be Viceroy of Kiangsu.

A new position, proud and dominating

We must be merciful. Advance opinion suggests some addicts may be treated for withdrawal. First surgery then medicine. Same with the Fanqui. Now they've surrendered all their Shit, I'm sending food and drink. We have so much to learn from one another: we of their machines, they of our mercy.

A great burst of gunfire. Lin does not react

Victoria appears from the smoke as Miss Fortune

Victoria June tenth, eighteen forty, the task force of fifteen warships joined us up the coast with five armed steamers of The Company and the *Cutty Sark* as a troop-carrier.

Dick appears, elegant but war-like

Dick The officers told us of Mama and Obadiah being nearly starved, of all our merchandise destroyed. We vowed to give the Chinks a bloody nose.

More guns

Lin (*unaware*) The hand of peace will show our strength and moderation all at once.

Sally appears, now dull and wasted, eyes dark

Sally The people of Ting-Hai saw our clipper moored off shore and word went round we'd brought the best quality poppy—which I can certainly endorse—so that they prepared to welcome us with open arms.

Dick The cruisers let off broadsides for nine minutes by my watch.

Victoria Sally sat on deck staring with glassy eyes at the burning town.

Sally A garden of orange flowers flaming on the water ... (*she swigs laudanum*)

Dick I was glad when Miss Fortune ordered her ashore.

Sally A diorama of blood and flames ...

Gunfire

Victoria Let's about God's work, girl. As a nurse, she was practically useless. We might have converted twice as many souls that day, had she not become so languid.

Lin I shall spend these twenty days of the burning writing lines on the theme: Of all household objects the looking-glass is the most wise.

Gunfire

Dick Gotcha!

The chorus sing "Burning, burning now" × 8 while Dick speaks

(*Speaking*)   Brave lads, you've had a good time in Ting-Hai
                 But in the south are bigger fish to fry.
                 All hands on deck, cast off for Canton now
                 Where we shall teach the Chinese to Kow-tow!

Music 15: Kow-tow

Voice 1   What's the hottest dance around?
Voice 2   Setting fire to the town?

Voice 3	You can't dig it if you're proud
Voice 4	So surrender, join the crowd,
Voice 5	Asian, Western——
Voice 6	Tory, whig
Voice 7	Hands together,
All	come and learn this jig

Chorus
First you go down on your knees
Knock your head—that's bound to please.
That is how
To do the Kow-tow.

Stand and take three paces more,
Three more times knock on the floor.
High brow, low brow
Do the Kow-tow
Kow-tow, everybody kow-tow.
Kow-tow, everybody kow-tow.
Every moo-cow
Gee-gee, bow-wow,
Poles in Kraków,
Reds in Moscow,
German hausfrau,
Black-faced Mau-Mau,
Brave in pow-wow,
Learn to bow now

Dick Do the kow-tow.
Chorus Do the kow-tow.

It became an Eastern dance sensation
When the Chinese taught it to the rest:
Steps like these come easy to the Asian;
No-one seems to do them in the West.

Dick
Three more paces to advance,
Knock knock knock to end the dance,
Then—and how!—
You'll make the Kow-tow.
Then—and how!—
You'll make the Kow-tow.
Kow-tow everybody kow-tow
Kow-tow everybody kow-tow.

*Lin comes dressed for war, waving a sword in martial manner. Dick avoids
all his gestures and finally stops all Lin's show with a great burst of gunfire.
Lin falls, rubs the imperial ring but fails to produce the Emperor. Lin
makes Kow-tow. Dick sings on*

All the villages from Canton to the sea
Are burning, burning, burning now,
Burning, burning, burning now

Burning, burning, burning now
Burning, burning, burning now
Burning to be free

SCENE 10

Peking

A gauze drops covering the warship

With a small explosion like a damp squib, the Emperor appears from a trap-door, slowly, he climbs out and a spotlight finds him. Lin is near him, kow-towing, stripped of his splendour

Emperor Commissioner Lin I hope you bring good news. What is the meaning of this last dispatch, suggesting I should listen to their terms?
Lin Their warships have destroyed our ports. They're cruising up the river to Canton.
Emperor You told me our defences can't be breached.
Lin We see the savages are strong.
Emperor You told me we were stronger.
Lin Our marines are disappointing.
Emperor Our marines are never beaten.
Lin Perhaps not by the enemy.
Emperor By what then?
Lin Seasickness.
Emperor Canton's a hundred miles *inland.*
Lin But our marines are seasick *on the river.*
Emperor Then find a cure.
Lin We know the cure.
Emperor What is it?
Lin Smoking *poppy.*
Emperor How can they fight in such a dream?
Lin They can't. They all deserted.
Emperor (*crying out*) Get them back!

Lin goes out backwards

The Emperor begins a series of illusions using the scroll to produce silks, flowers, etc. From under his cloak he brings a balloon with a savage tiger's head on it but it bursts and he holds up the limp shreds of rubber. Bringing out a pack of cards he appeals to the audience

Take a card, any card, come on . . .

He shuffles the pack but fumbles and they fall, attached to each other on a string

Lin comes back, not kow-towing now and more casual in his approach

Lin Majesty . . .

Emperor Commissioner Lin, good news, I hope?
Lin Our great and awesome Admiral Kuan—
Emperor Direct descendant of the god of war?
Lin The same—has sold his uniform.
Emperor He's what?
Lin To bribe each man to stay on board the ships. Their pay is not enough to live on.
Emperor Then how do they survive?
Lin By smuggling poppy.
Emperor (*to him*) Take a card. Any card. (*He offers him a new pack*) What price our ancient cannon breathing fire?
Lin The fire cannot reach the British ships.
Emperor Pick a card. Look at it. Put it back.

Lin does; the Emperor shuffles

It's time to use those monkeys with lighted torches on their tails to go aboard and blow up all their powder magazines.
Lin Majesty, their ships are made of steel.
Emperor What's that when it's home?
Lin We aren't too sure. We know it can't be burnt or blown up.
Emperor That's your card.
Lin (*looking*) No.

The Emperor shuffles again

Poison! Why not poison?
Lin Someone tried it in the siege.
Emperor Then send the kind of food they like. Whole cows and pigs—
Lin All poisoned?
Emperor No! Your card.
Lin (*looking*) Closer.
Emperor (*shuffling again*) Wait till they begin to suffer with the gripes. Their groans will turn to cries, their cries to screams but we'll withhold the only antidote.
Lin Sire, they don't depend on rhubarb.
Emperor No? Then what?
Lin (*shrugging*) Accept their terms.
Emperor Makee-mark chop-chop. Sign now. Quibble later. The quickness of the hand deceives the eye. Your card.
Lin No.

Sadly Lin shakes his head and goes, turning his back

Emperor puts away cards and from the rolled scroll produces a dead rabbit. Tries to slap it into life, fails. Gathers his props and goes as:

Dick comes on to ask the audience to boo and hiss him

SCENE 11

Treaty scene

The scrim flies and we are on the warship's deck

Dodo and Upward enter and are reunited with Dick and the crew, who now give three rousing cheers

We see that a table and chairs are upstage and Dick leaps on to the table and, as the music ends, a fanfare is played

Upward Dick, the Mandarins are due on board to sign the treaty and we need an interpreter. Where's Miss Fortune?
Dick Saving souls among the Cantonese.
Upward What about Sally, wasn't she getting up the lingo?
Dick Well, she *was* but since Ting-Hai she's hardly shown her face.

Jack climbs from a trap-door leading Sally from below-ships. She's bent and frail, as though in a fever

Dodo Sally, my dear, how are you? Dick says you've not been well.

Sally cries out as Dodo approaches her, hides behind Jack

Jack She is a little poorly, yes.
Upward So help me bob.
Sally I'll be all right, only keep that creature away from me.
Dodo Oh, charming. Really!
Sally I've got some medicine here will make me right as rain.

Jack takes her laudanum flask as she tries to drink

Jack Afterwards, gal.
Dick We want you to interpret for us.
Sally What? The ways of God to man?

She giggles like a child. Everyone watches silently

Dick Some other time perhaps. I meant—
Sally But not the ways of man to man. Who *could*?
Jack I think they mean the treaty terms.

A sound of piping aboard gives warning of the Mandarins' approach. The British arrange themselves behind the tables as in a formal Victorian photograph

In silence Lin and the Chinese come in from the stalls

The Brits glower. Reaching a place near the table, the Chinese start to perform the kow-tow

Dick (*impatiently*) Now, none of that, I beg you, sirs. The usual salutation in our country is a bow.

Sally takes this up and repeats it to the Chinese. Dick says all she says first.

That's the form for the next dialogue. Lin and the Chinese stand and awkwardly bow

Dick Now tell them they had better hear the terms.
Sally Now hear the treaty terms.
Dick And be it known there's no negotiating. No quibbling, no arguing the point.

Sally repeats

The only argument that means a fig is sixteen cruisers standing off Canton. Your forts guarding the city are destroyed, your fleet is sunk. Our guns are on Canton——
Sally —and if you balk they'll make a blaze as delicate as sweet-scented orange roses embraced by a smiling naked virgin—sweet as the delicious blood of Jesus Christ, our Lord—who came to earth to loot and kill and ravish us all for his name's sake—
Dodo Has she got it right do you think?
Sally The island was a show ground of gorgeous tableaux vivants.
Jack Sally, love, just say what they say—

Music 15C: The Treaty

Sally (*singing*) A diorama of blood and flames.
Dodo The Chinamen are starting.
Dick Something's wrong.
Sally (*singing*) Here a surgeon of the navy finds a village girl who has killed herself in fear. He cuts off her tiny bound feet for his collection of curios.
Dick I said she'd not been well ...
Sally (*singing*) There were some Chinese women hiding up a tree like so many rooks in a rookery. Some of our sailors find great sport in firing up at them—there is a sort of beauty in their fall—head first, bleeding most profusely.
Dick Get her below, Jack.
Sally Yes, please ... medicine and peace ... and pretty pictures ... one of Christ with a bayonet ... he pitched a Chinese boy into a burning house ...

Jack gives her the flask and she drinks as they go

Pause. Upward smiles

Upward Velly solly. Missee plentee sick.

Victoria enters

Victoria Sorry I'm late. I've done it into their lingo.
Dick Capital.

A chord is struck and the following is spoken monotonously like a chant over music

Chinese Item One: We undertake to pay two million dollars damages.

Upward That's two followed by half a dozen noughts.
Dick In Spanish silver.
Victoria Item Two.
Chinese The ports will be opened to foreign trade——
Dick With consuls everywhere and access to the Mandarins.
Victoria Item Three.
Chinese We give you Hong Kong Island—
Dick Where we can build an offshore base—
Upward To supply the treaty ports with merchandise.
Dodo And we won't let them have it back in a hurry, will we, boys and girls?
Victoria Item Four.
Chinese Of all the guests, we see you as Most Favoured Nation.
Dick Means Number One, you savvy?

As the Chinese sign . . .

Dodo To which you put your hands, at the hour of the horse.
Dick On the day of the tiger.
Upward In the Year of the Rat—
All For ever and ever. Amen.

Guns are heard. Lin and the Mandarins cower in fear. The British laugh

Dick They make kow-tow. Twenty-one plenty big bang kow-tow.

Dick, Victoria and Upward go, contented

Lin remains alone

The Emperor creeps on, making sure Dick has gone

Emperor I trusted you. You gave them Hong Kong. What punishment can I devise to fit this crime? Strangling won't be nearly good enough.
Lin Long before the Fanqui we had gunpowder. We knew magnetic compasses before they had sails.
Emperor You will not be Viceroy after all.
Lin Two thousand years ago we had the turbine.
Emperor Return my ring. You're not Commissioner.

Lin drops the ring into his hand

You're exiled to the North West. Your property is confiscated. Go!
Lin (*to him*) And that won't save the Manchu dynasty.

Lin goes

Victoria comes on

The Emperor rolls a copy of the treaty

Victoria That man you exiled, by his very failure, helped to found Hong Kong. The Mecca of free trade.
Emperor The clippers followed swiftly on the gun-boats, yes. (*He shows us the scroll is empty, then produces poppies from it, strewing them over the stage*)

Victoria We answered a demand. You couldn't stamp it out once it had started.

Emperor I'd stamped it out before you came.

Victoria You vexing man, no modern trading nation can possibly survive in isolation.

Emperor Your engines are irrelevant. Your toys mean nothing.

Victoria Hong Kong's become a wonder of the world!

Emperor Hong Kong, nineteen seventy, more than half the people hooked.

Victoria Milton Friedman's favourite place!

Emperor Not to mention heroin, base morphine, amphetamine.

SCENE 12

Chinese Takeaway

Victoria loses patience and stamps off

Emperor tips the rest of the poppy petals over the audience and goes as:

> *Dodo and Upward enter, encouraging the audience to boo and hiss*

Dodo Come on boys and girls, I want to hear it loud and clear.

Upward You've always had a nostalgia for it, haven't you?

Dodo What?

Upward The boo.

Dodo Well he deserves it.

Upward Oh, he does. We trusted him. Being Englishmen. We took it for granted he'd keep his word.

Dodo When a Chinaman gives you his word—forget it!

Upward During the next twenty years they wiped their arses on our treaty so often we finally had to march with the French army to Peking and there, to give the Chinks a hiding they should not forget, we sacked the Summer Palace.

Front tabs come in

Music 16: Chinese Takeaway

Both	From the paradise of countless trees
	Old Lasting Glory's flown;
	The mighty ruler of the seven seas
	Has left the Dragon throne.
Upward	A British tommy
Dodo	And a frog
Both	Shout a sort of catalogue
	Of every antique they throw
	To their waiting mates below.
Dodo	Jacques, I've shot the peacocks
	So we'll dine on *coq au vin*,
Upward	Tommy, catch this music-box
	And diamond-studded fan.

Dodo	Jacques, this is a dragon from The Son of 'eaven's throne;
Upward	Chuck this clock in the wagon, Tom, It's made of precious stone.
Both	Our officer's orders are to break Anything here we cannot take— The sound you hear's the fusiliers Shooting the crystal chandeliers— Rat-tat-tat-tat!

Chorus

Rat-a-tat-tat-tat! Ker-pow-splatt!
　　Rat-a-tat-tat-tat!
Rat-a-tat-tat-tat! Ker-pow-splatt!
　　Rat-a-tat-tat-tat!
Hip-hooray, what a frabjous day—
And the whites don't have to pay.
Did you ever see such a succulent dish of
　　Chinese takeaway?

Upward	Before we smashed the furniture And set the place ablaze,
Dodo	We took away the silk and fur And sang the Marseillaise. We took away the intricately carved chiffonier—
Both	Oh, you couldn't wish for a tastier dish of Chinese takeaway?

Chorus

Rat-tat-tat-tat! Ker-pow-splatt! Rat-tat-tat-tat!
Rat-tat-tat-tat! Ker-pow-splatt! Rat-tat-tat-tat!
Hip-hooray, what a frabjous day—
And the whites don't have to pay.
Oh, you couldn't wish
For a tastier dish of
Chinese takeaway!

Songsheet scene

Dodo Oh, that was lovely, I did enjoy that, let's do it again.
Upward Why?
Dodo Because the finale's not ready yet, that's why.
Upward Well, if we're going to do it again, we're going to need some help
　　from the boys and girls out there.
Dodo Idle, turn up the house lights.

The house Lights come up

Upward Swelp me bob! Turn them off, for gawd's sake.
Dodo Now come on, boys and girls, you're going to enjoy this. Thank you,
　　Professor.

They start to sing

Stop, stop, stop.

Upward What's wrong with the boys and girls?

Dodo Maybe they don't know the words.

Upward Don't know the words. Idle! The laundry list please.

A songsheet is flown in

Oh you are clever Dorothea.

Dodo Now you've got the words, you can sing. Thank you, Professor.

They start but ...

Oh, oh, oh, oh.

Upward Hallo, the rhubarb's working.

Dodo No, I've just had the most marvellous original idea—let's have a competition. Let's divide the boys and girls in two—I'll have the boys and girls this side and we'll do the Rat-tat-tat-tats.

Upward And I'll take the boys and girls this side and we'll do the Ker-pow-splatts.

Dodo And we'll divide them down the middle, so all those on this side of that man with the big red nose and ginger moustache—oh, I'm awfully sorry, madam. I do apologize—we'll do the Rat-tat-tat-tats.

Upward And my side, we'll reply with Ker-pow-splatts.

They sing through the song

Oh, oh, oh, I've had an even better idea than yours. Let's do it with actions. Now ker-pow-splatt sounds like a grenade being thrown—Ker-pow-splatt. That's what we'll do.

Dodo Yes and when we do Rat-tat-tat-tats, we can all pretend that we've got Gatling guns. Rat-tat-tat-tat. And let's all do it to them, shall we?

Upward And we will do it to them. Let's do what our wonderful soldiers did to the Summer Palace and ...

Both Take the roof off. Thank you, Professor.

They sing through the song

Dodo and Upward exit

The songsheet flies

Scene 13

Finale

Jack enters

Jack   All true. No fairy-tale. Not just a song.
They sacked the palace, occupied Hong Kong,
Made it an offshore base for trade so vast
One British newspaper could claim at last
Nine out of ten among the Cantonese
Depended on the poppy for their ease.

> The merchants, once they felt they'd made
>   enough,
> Handed the trade to others just as rough
> And sailed to England, served on City boards,
> Built palaces, became MPs and lords,
> "Once upon a time" has now become
> "Happy Ever After". Well, for some——

He turns to one side as:

> *Sally enters in an invalid chair. Her face is ashen, her gums blackened, her hair lifeless, hanging loose*

Jack kneels by her and smooths back her hair, caresses her cheek. He turns again to us

> Next week we shall be hazarding our fates
> Across the ocean, sailing for the States,
> For folk like us, the new world's full of hope,
> Free maybe, but above all free of dope!

A fanfare and the CURTAIN *rises on a palace with chandeliers and, up centre, a grand staircase. Couples are waltzing to "Nostalgie de la boue". Jack and Sally stand aside watching. Then all the principals come down for their bows, including Lin and the Emperor and Randy with a halo, and line up awaiting Dick. Dodo's a bride, Upward a groom*

Footman's Voice My lords, ladies and gentlemen, pray silence for Sir Richard and Lady Whittington.

Everyone cheers, confetti falls from flies. Everyone turns as:

> *Dick appears in modern morning suit and top hat with a previously unseen girl in bridal dress*

Dick   Dick Whittington's once more become Lord
>   Mayor
> And not a sign of pussy anywhere!
> I've come to occupy the Mansion House
> With Obadiah's daughter as my spouse.

Cheers, they kiss

> Merging our mutual interests in one
> Great PLC called Upward-Whittington.
Upward   As you can see, I've got into the gentry
> By using what-I-call the tradesman's entry.

He pats Dodo's behind, she slaps his hand

Dodo   In looking at each blushing bride and groom,
> You may be wondering which does what to
>   whom.
Upward   Well, now you mention it——
Dodo   Let me explain:
> We form a sort of daisy chain.

Victoria	*(at the top of the stairs)* My company's *un*limited. Its trade Embraces Aberdeen and Adelaide, A family in which we all can dare Meet without kowtow Mandarin and Mayor.
Upward	And even Queen Victoria——God bless'er!
Dick	So now——on with the dance——
All	Thank you, Professor!

Music 17: Bounty of the Earth *(Reprise)*

(Singing)

Rejoice! For Harvest Home.
Oh, see the generous crops!
From limits far as man can roam
Replenishing the shops,
Grateful retailers
Calculate its worth
How can it fail us?
The Bounty of the Earth.
Amen.

After the pantomime walk-down and finale bows they sing a reprise of
"Blessed Trinity"

Music 18: Blessed Trinity *(Reprise)*

All *(singing)*

That's civilisation, commerce and Christianity
All go together and begin with a C
Got to deliver that heathen hoard
So come on children get on board
The ship that's chartered by the Lord
That's the blessed, the blessed, the blessed
Blessed Trinity
The Blessed Trinity.

CURTAIN

FURNITURE AND PROPERTY LIST

ACT I

SCENE 1

On stage: Throne

Personal: **Emperor:** magic tricks
Victoria: orb and sceptre

SCENE 2

On stage: Statue
Well
Tree. *Behind it:* xylophone

Off stage: Saddle (**Jack**)

Personal: **Dodo:** gun
Dick: riding crop

SCENE 3

On stage: Desks. *On them:* quill pens, ledgers, abacuses, money
Chairs
Oil portraits
Chandeliers

Off stage: Address book (**Dodo**)

Personal: **Dick:** IOU

SCENE 4

On stage: Ship behind scrim
Throne

SCENE 5

On stage: Costumes

Off stage: Stick (**Sally**)
Howdah on baby elephant (**Dodo**)
Drinks (**Bearers**)
Food for elephant (**Servants**)

Personal: **Dodo:** smoking gun
Upward: gun

SCENE 6

On stage: Chests of opium
Table. *On it:* hammer

SCENE 7

On stage: Chests of opium on shelves and floor
Bed of straw
3-legged stool
Bucket of food
Lamp

Off stage: Bag containing small box, bamboo pipe, box of matches, spoon-headed
needle **(Dick)**
Trapeze for transformation scene (page 28) **(Stage Management)**

Personal: **Randy:** ice-pack on head, equine thermometer in mouth
Jack: fob watch

ACT II

SCENE 1

On stage: Throne, flash bombs for **Emperor**

Personal: **Emperor:** ring

SCENE 2

On stage: Thrones
Gong and striker

Personal: **Lin:** scroll
Guards: swords

SCENE 3

Off stage: Cart piled with laundry bags

Personal: **Jack:** mouth-organ
Sally: parasol, laudanum flask

SCENE 4

On stage: Desks
Chairs
Chandeliers

Off stage: Glass of fluid **(Sally)**

Personal: **Victoria:** umbrella

SCENE 5

No props required

SCENE 6

On stage: High wall
               Garden seat
               Flagpole with British flag

Off stage: Cart with bundles of bibles and hymn-books tied with string **(Randy)**
               Bibles **(Jack)**
               Severed head on pole, dripping blood **(Stage Management)**
               Bibles, luggage, chests with opium balls **(Clerks)**
               Severed head **(Stage Management)**
               Severed head **(Stage Management)**
               More bibles, luggage **(Clerks)**
               2 severed heads on poles **(Stage Management)**
               Sealed letter **(Upward)**
               Severed head on pole **(Stage Management)**
               3 more severed heads on poles **(Stage Management)**
               Apples, oranges, cabbages **(Stage Management)**
               Severed head **(Stage Management)**

Personal: **Jack:** handkerchief, ocarina
              Sally: laudanum flask

SCENE 7

On stage: As Scene 6

Off stage: Carrot on stick **(Jack)**

Personal: **Jack:** pistol

SCENE 8

On stage: As Scene 6, plus:
               6 Chinese heads on poles
               Flag removed from pole

Off stage: Flag **(Dodo)**
               Head on pole **(Stage Management)**

SCENE 9

On stage: Deck of warship

Personal: **Lin:** fan, ring
              Sally: laudanum flask

SCENE 10

On stage: Nil

Personal: **Emperor:** scroll, magic tricks including 2 packs cards, silks, flowers,
              balloons, dead rabbit

SCENE 11

On stage: Table. *On it:* treaty, pen, ink
            Chairs

Off stage: Songsheet **(Stage Management)**

Personal: **Sally:** laudanum flask
            Lin: ring
            Emperor: trick poppies

SCENE 12

No props required

LIGHTING PLOT

Property fittings required: chandeliers

ACT I, SCENE 1

To open: Swirling mass of water effect

Cue 1   As music takes on oriental tinge   (Page 1)
            Bring up lighting behind scrim

ACT I, SCENE 2

To open: General exterior lighting

Cue 2   **Sally:** "There, there, Cherry, never mind."   (Page 5)
            Red spot on **Cherry** *for a few moments*

ACT I, SCENE 3

To open: Interior lighting, chandeliers on

Cue 3   **Clerks:** "Upward Upward"   (Page 10)
            Spot on **Upward** *at main desk*

Cue 4   At end of Song 4   (Page 12)
            Fade spot

ACT I, SCENE 4

To open: Lighting behind scrim

Cue 5   As ship makes its way across   (Page 15)
            Storm effects—lightning, etc.

Cue 6   As **Emperor** appears   (Page 15)
            Lightning

Cue 7   **Emperor** creates lightning   (Page 15)
            Lightning

ACT I, SCENE 5

To open: General exterior lighting

No cues

ACT I, SCENE 6

To open: General interior lighting

No cues

ACT I, SCENE 7

To open: Lightning

Cue 8	As frontcloth rises *Dim realistic lighting*	(Page 26)
Cue 9	As **Dick**, **Sally** and **Jack** continue to smoke *Lights change for transformation scene*	(Page 28)
Cue 10	As Music 8 ends *Lights fade, then come up on advertisement frontcloth. Then House lights up*	(Page 29)

ACT II, SCENE 1

To open: General lighting

No cues

ACT II, SCENE 2

To open: General lighting

Cue 1	**Lin** rubs ring on finger *Image of* **Emperor** *appears*	(Page 34)
Cue 2	**Emperor:** ". . . with the Vermilion Pencil!" *Lightning*	(Page 34)
Cue 3	**Lin** prostrates himself before **Emperor**'s image *Fade image*	(Page 34)

ACT II, SCENE 3

To open: General lighting

No cues

ACT II, SCENE 4

To open: General interior lighting

No cues

ACT II, SCENE 5

To open: General interior lighting

No cues

ACT II, SCENE 6

To open: General exterior lighting

No cues

ACT II, SCENE 7
To open: Exterior lighting—nearing sunset
No cues

ACT II, SCENE 8
To open: Bright morning light
No cues

ACT II, SCENE 9
To open: General lighting
No cues

ACT II, SCENE 10
To open: Lighting DS in front of scrim
Cue 4   As **Emperor** climbs out trap-door   (Page 54)
     Spot on him

ACT II, SCENE 11
To open: General lighting on deck
Cue 5   **Dodo:** "... turn up the house lights."   (Page 60)
     House lights up

ACT II, SCENE 12
To open: General lighting
No cues

EFFECTS PLOT

ACT I

ACT II